Taking the Lead

The United Nations and Population Assistance

Shanti R. Conly
Population Action International

Acknowledgments

When Population Action International (PAI) embarked on this study with the aim of promoting a better understanding of the role of the United Nations (UN) in population activities, I did not fully comprehend the ambitious scope of the project or my own lack of knowledge of the UN system. A year later, I am acutely conscious of how much I still have to learn. This report owes its strengths and virtues to the generous help of people inside and outside the UN system. Its faults, of course, are my own.

I owe a special debt to those UN agencies which provided PAI with relevant information. In particular, staff at the United Nations Population Fund gave graciously of their time and responded with openness to endless requests for information.

The report draws heavily on the work of Cynthia Green, who as a consultant to PAI prepared a companion piece, *Profiles of UN Organizations Working in Population*. Cynthia's research laid much of the groundwork for the present report.

I am enormously grateful to the many colleagues who patiently educated me on the work of the United Nations in the population field. Among others who provided valuable perspective through interviews or comments on early drafts, Maggie Catley-Carlson, Dick Cornelius, Barbara Crane, Judy Harrington, Steve Mendelsohn, Tom Merrick, Steve Sinding and Joe Wheeler all made major substantive contributions. Several PAI staff read, reread, and helped edit numerous drafts of the report. Finally, Karen Helsing of PAI provided invaluable research support and prepared the charts and tables for the report.

Table of Contents

Table of Contents iii

Executive Summary v

I. The United Nations and World Population 1

- 1945 to 1995: The UN Contribution to the Population Field 1
- The ICPD: Challenges and Emerging Needs 2
- The Case for Stronger UN Leadership in Population Assistance ... 2
- Political and Financial Constraints on UN Leadership 4
- Objectives of PAI's Report 5

II. UNFPA: Responding to the Needs of the 21st Century 7

- The Importance of UNFPA in UN Population Activities 7
- UNFPA's Mission and Achievements 7
- Extending UNFPA's Leadership from the Global to the Country Level 9
- Challenges for the 21st Century 9
    1. Increasing Global Funding for Population Programs 10
    2. Enhancing Country Level Strategic Leadership: Becoming "Chief Population Advisor" 15
    3. Thinking Big: Increasing the Impact of UNFPA Country Programs 18
    4. Meeting the Technical Assistance Needs of the 21st Century 24
    5. Addressing the Growing Demand for Contraceptive Supplies 28
    6. Staffing for Success: Strengthening Operational Capacity 31

III. Building Synergy within the UN System 37

- The Role of UNFPA in Interagency Coordination 37
- Progress and Constraints Relating to Interagency Collaboration 37
- Implementing ICPD: UNFPA and the Role of Other UN Agencies 39
    1. Strengthening Reproductive Health and Family Planning: Collaborating with WHO and UNICEF 39
    2. Enhancing Links Between Population, Women and Development: Complementing the Work of Other UN Agencies 43
    3. Creating a Global Consensus on Population: Working with the UN Policy Machinery 46

IV. The United States and UN Population Activities 50

V. Prospects for the Future 53

Key References. 54

Charts and Tables

UNFPA Expenditures, 1971-1995 8
Government Contributions from
    All Countries to UNFPA, 1971-1995 11
Major Donor Country Contributions to UNFPA, 1993-1995 12

Distribution of UNFPA Programs by Budget Size, 1994 & 1995 19
Implications of New UNFPA Resource Allocation Criteria 20
Allocation of UNFPA Assistance by Major Program Area, 1995.......................21
Trends in Management of UNFPA Programs 25
UNFPA Staff by Category and Location, 1996 31
UN Organizations Involved in Population Activities..36
U.S. Funding for UNFPA, U.S. Fiscal Years 1968-1996......................................50

Executive Summary

The United Nations: Meeting the Cairo Challenge

On the eve of the 21st century, population programs around the world face new challenges and new opportunities. The consensus reached by 180 nations in Cairo in 1994, at the International Conference on Population and Development (ICPD), revitalized and broadened support for these programs. At the same time, the comprehensive human development strategy agreed on at the ICPD requires that most developing countries make vast new investments in health and education. To meet ICPD goals for the expansion and improvement of family planning and other reproductive health services, many poor countries need external financial and technical assistance. Yet, while resource needs are rising, the leadership and financial support historically provided by the United States in the population field seem likely to decline.

In this changing environment, the United Nations (UN) appears the most appropriate institution to assume leadership in global population assistance. From the developing countries' perspective, the UN is a more politically neutral source of funds and advice than bilateral aid agencies. The UN has a worldwide network of country offices, and more than 20 UN entities are engaged in population activities, encompassing a wealth of specialized expertise. The UN has made important contributions to the population field and, in recent years, has served as a channel for roughly a third of grant aid to population programs — primarily in donor support to the United Nations Population Fund (UNFPA).

Concerns about the effectiveness of the overall UN system, however, call into question the potential for a stronger UN role on population issues. Many observers perceive the policy machinery established to guide the UN's development work as ineffective and regard the central UN Secretariat and UN specialized agencies as overgrown and inefficient. While the various development programs and funds — including UNFPA — are more effective, their activities are nonetheless characterized by fragmentation, duplication, and weak coordination.

UNFPA: Responding to the Needs of the 21st Century

Despite the proliferation of UN entities working in population, UNFPA is the key player at an operational level. It is the only UN organization directly assisting countries in implementing the ICPD action plan on reproductive health and family planning. The Fund provides population assistance to more countries than any other bilateral or multilateral donor and is the sole source of such assistance in several countries. By supporting the population work of other UN organizations, it can also promote broader linkages between population and development throughout the UN system.

As its leadership of the ICPD process has shown, UNFPA has been especially successful as a global advocate for population and family planning programs and, increasingly, for efforts to improve the status of women. The ICPD has given UNFPA a fresh mandate — and new energy and direction. Nonetheless, at the country level, the Fund has not fully realized its potential for impact in either of its two main roles — as an adviser on strategic policy issues, or as a source of technical and financial support to population programs. UNFPA's principal challenge, then, is to replicate its global leadership in individual countries.

The gap between UNFPA's impact and potential at the country level

UNFPA's principal challenge is to replicate its global leadership in individual countries.

largely reflects the limitations of funds and staff, relative to the number of countries requesting assistance and the scope of their needs. UNFPA, nevertheless, can take a number of steps to strengthen its leadership and programs; indeed, it has already initiated changes aimed at improving its impact. At the same time, other UN organizations must do more to support the ICPD goals and the work of UNFPA.

Initially a vehicle for raising funds for population projects implemented by other UN agencies, the Fund has over the years assumed an expanded and more direct role in program implementation. As UNFPA seeks to support national efforts to implement the ICPD *Programme of Action*, it needs to further strengthen its operational effectiveness. Specifically, it must address the following challenges if it is to continue to respond in a dynamic way to the changing international population assistance scene and the evolving needs in developing countries.

■ **UNFPA must further expand its role in mobilizing global financing for population programs and in helping countries secure the resources they need for ICPD implementation.** UNFPA is the only organization that can advocate for increased population funding with both donor and developing country governments. At the global level, UNFPA has helped to mobilize increased donor country contributions to population programs, but resources remain inadequate. UNFPA needs to further strengthen its advocacy to increase contributions from lagging donor countries as well as long-time donors in the field, both for its own programs and for population assistance more generally. At the country level, too, the Fund should assume a more central and catalytic role in advising governments on the mobilization of domestic financial resources, and in helping countries coordinate and secure increased donor assistance.

■ **The Fund must assume a stronger leadership role on policy issues at the country level, in essence, becoming the "chief population adviser" to governments.** The ICPD gave UNFPA an important mandate to help national governments reshape population policies and programs. To play this role, UNFPA country representatives must have the stature and expertise to provide sound and strategic policy advice and more consistently facilitate the development of national plans relating to ICPD implementation. Stronger analytical and technical work must support UNFPA efforts to exert greater intellectual leadership and influence on policy. Closer collaboration with the World Bank, with its analytical capacity and influence on governments, would also strengthen UNFPA's engagement in and impact on policy discussions.

■ **For greater impact, the Fund needs to allocate resources more strategically to countries and program areas.** UNFPA represents a significant source of financial support to help developing countries implement the ICPD *Programme of Action*. Yet its 1995 program budget of $289 million was spread thinly across 150 countries. Within countries, limited resources have been splintered across many program areas and small projects. UNFPA has developed new criteria for allocating funds and redefined core program areas, but these efforts have not adequately addressed the dispersion of resources. The Fund needs to focus its funds on fewer countries, selecting countries where it can have an impact in achieving ICPD goals and where its financial assistance is significant relative to that of other donors. Within countries,

UNFPA is the only organization that can advocate for increased population funding with both donor and developing country governments.

UNFPA needs to better identify strategic priorities and overhaul its programming approach to transform the current agglomeration of small projects into more coherent assistance programs. To enhance program effectiveness, UNFPA should also expand support for private sector institutions and strengthen evaluation of program impact.

■ **UNFPA needs to become the primary source of state-of-the-art technical expertise to help developing countries expand and improve reproductive health and family planning services.** In the past, other UN agencies directly managed UNFPA-funded projects. As UNFPA country offices and national governments have increasingly assumed responsibility for project management, UNFPA has established regional teams of experts from different UN organizations to provide technical support to country programs. The new system has improved support to UNFPA-funded projects, increased accountability and reduced costs. However, it still draws too much on other UN entities, many of which lack cutting edge population expertise. Over the long term, UNFPA needs to expand partnerships outside the UN system, moving towards new technical support arrangements where NGOs and other private sector groups can compete for global or regional technical assistance contracts. The Fund must also do more to support the development of NGO and private sector expertise within developing countries.

■ **UNFPA needs to further strengthen its capacity to meet the growing requirements for contraceptive supplies arising from the worldwide expansion of family planning efforts.** The Fund's commodity assistance has grown dramatically in the past several years, through both UNFPA-funded procurements and the provision of procurement services to help governments and other donors with bulk contraceptive purchases. UNFPA has recently taken steps to strengthen the efficiency and responsiveness of its procurement systems. Overall, however, the Fund has not addressed the increased need for contraceptive supplies in a sufficiently bold and vigorous way. UNFPA's Executive Board should increase the recently approved revolving fund so that the procurement unit can shift to a system of anticipating needs and placing consolidated advance orders. UNFPA also needs to expand its in-house procurement expertise and to develop new technical assistance arrangements with external institutions to help countries build their own capacity to manage their contraceptive supply needs.

■ **To address the challenges identified above, UNFPA needs to strengthen its staff capacity.** UNFPA professional staff, particularly its field staff, have been stretched very thin, limiting the Fund's capacity for effective program monitoring and implementation. Field offices have relied heavily on country directors, who are supported primarily by national staff as a cost-savings measure. In a positive step, in late 1995, UNFPA's Executive Board approved a large number of new field positions for locally hired support staff. However, UNFPA needs to further strengthen field office professional staffing. If UNFPA concentrated funds in fewer countries, it could redeploy staff to these countries to enhance managerial and technical capacity. In addition, it may need to recruit more mid-level professional staff, including some international staff who can help transfer successful program experiences across countries.

UNFPA headquarters in New York has roughly a fourth of the Fund's

Over the long term, UNFPA needs to expand partnerships outside the UN system.

UN organizations need to strengthen their collaboration in the population field.

total staff, but headquarters personnel spend too much time on UN conferences and coordination meetings. The Fund's leadership needs to reorder priorities and shift the focus of headquarters staff to supporting UNFPA country programs. Professional staff at headquarters, moreover, are distributed across a variety of functions. The Fund should explore options for restructuring, including increasing professional positions relative to support staff, and consolidating organizational units to allow greater depth of expertise in key program areas. UNFPA also needs to expand training and reward good performance. Professional staff should rotate regularly between New York and the field.

Building Synergies within the UN System

Given limited resources, UNFPA needs to establish strategic alliances with other UN organizations, to maximize support for the broader ICPD social agenda. However, UNFPA's ability to forge effective partnerships is constrained by the capacity and commitment of other UN entities.

The UN system has made a concerted effort in recent years to improve coordination of both development and population activities at the country level. Nevertheless, the UN's development efforts lack central oversight and coordination. At the country level, UN organizations still develop programs separately in a piecemeal approach. The ICPD has been a catalytic force promoting increased dialogue within the system, yet most UN organizations lack a deep commitment to population activities.

Solutions to some of these problems require far ranging reforms of the UN system. Even in the absence of such reform, UN organizations could take a number of steps to strengthen their collaboration in the population field.

■ **In reproductive health and family planning, the World Health Organization (WHO) and the United Nations Children's Fund (UNICEF) need to become more effective partners with UNFPA at the country level.** As the lead technical agency in reproductive health within the UN, WHO's role is primarily to set international norms and disseminate information on new approaches. In recent years, it has provided significant leadership in contraceptive research, adolescent sexual health, safe motherhood and AIDS prevention. WHO has had very limited staff and funds to support country-level programs.

WHO recently reorganized its reproductive health activities at its headquarters in Geneva, with the aim of enhancing its capacity to advise UNFPA and national governments on the development of reproductive health programs. However, problems of coordination between WHO headquarters in Geneva and its largely independent regional offices undermine WHO's ability to serve as a strong partner to UNFPA in the field.

In contrast, UNICEF is a strong, operational organization with a large field presence. UNICEF's health, education and women's programs directly support the ICPD plan of action. UNICEF also has significant potential to play a greater role in reproductive health and family planning and has recently increased support for maternal and adolescent health programs. However, its primary emphasis has been on safe delivery and AIDS prevention, in part, reflecting long-standing political pressures to avoid involvement in family planning.

At the headquarters level, UNFPA and WHO, and to a lesser extent UNICEF, collaborate on reproductive health-related policy development and technical dialogue in a largely complementary way. At the country level, the organizations have relatively little direct program collaboration reflecting WHO's operational weakness and UNICEF's desire for operational autonomy. In some countries, WHO and UNICEF representatives are weak advocates for family planning and do not adequately coordinate with UNFPA.

High level consultations, beginning with top leadership, are needed for UNFPA, WHO and UNICEF to develop more mutually supportive working relationships. Both UNICEF and WHO have significant potential to influence health policy and must ensure more consistent advocacy for reproductive health and family planning by their field representatives. WHO should pursue current efforts to strengthen its capacity to provide technical support at the country level; if it proves unable to respond to UNFPA's needs, the Fund will need to look beyond the UN system for these services. Finally, there is enormous potential for UNICEF to expand joint programming with UNFPA, since in almost all respects its programs support ICPD goals and complement the work of UNFPA.

■ **The UN system needs a better division of labor with respect to women's development activities.** UN organizations must do more in their own areas to support women's programs. The ICPD saw women's empowerment as important to effective population programs. Together, the ICPD and Beijing conference on women provide a blueprint for the UN's work with women. However, the UN lacks coherent and strong institutions with political clout and resources to advance the women's development agenda.

In the absence of effective leadership within the UN system, UNFPA has emerged as one of the most vigorous advocates for women's empowerment. With its limited resources, the Fund will need to set clear boundaries between advocacy and large-scale support for women's programs. At the country level, UNFPA should vigorously promote women's programs as part of efforts to help plan for ICPD implementation and encourage other UN agencies to support women's development activities in their areas of expertise. It should reconsider existing partnerships with these agencies in reproductive health and family planning, where their overall comparative advantage is low.

■ **The international community needs to strengthen those elements of the UN's policy machinery which hold potential for stimulating increased national support for population programs.** The Economic and Social Council, which is responsible for overall coordination of UN development policy, has been weak and ineffective. The Commission on Population, traditionally responsible for overseeing the work of the Population Division in the UN Secretariat, was recently reconstituted as the Commission on Population and Development and has assumed the broader responsibility of monitoring ICPD implementation. The role of the Commission is evolving; UN member states and the NGO community must monitor its effectiveness and work to enhance its relevance and impact. Other UN functional commissions dealing with sustainable development and women's issues also have potential to bring population issues to the attention of a broader range of policymakers and integrate them into overall development debates.

The UN Population Division has played an important role in policy development through its demographic analyses and projections, which have enhanced awareness of population

Both UNICEF and WHO should be stronger advocates for reproductive health and family planning.

trends. Closer collaboration between UNFPA and the Population Division on an ongoing basis would strengthen the links between the UN's policy and operational work in population and the Division's reporting on operational programs to the Commission on Population and Development.

The series of international population conferences organized by the UN every 10 years has also been successful in stimulating political commitment to national population and family planning programs. The recent ICPD had a particularly strong influence on policy. In the absence of a more effective formal UN policy machinery, UNFPA will need to rely more on the international conference process and on direct outreach to national leaders on a continuing basis to influence national policies and funding for population programs.

The United States and UN Population Activities

U.S. leadership helped to create UNFPA, and until 1985 the United States was UNFPA's largest donor. The United States, with its substantial technical expertise on population issues, has also been influential on the Executive Board of UNFPA. These achievements were undermined in the mid-1980s when U.S. conservative groups attacked UNFPA for its presence in China, following allegations of widespread coercion resulting from China's one-child policy. This led to the withdrawal of U.S. financial support, even though an official report concluded that UNFPA did not support coercive family planning practices. In 1993, the United States restored support to UNFPA and went on to play a key role in the ICPD process. However, in 1996, congressionally mandated cuts in U.S. population assistance, including funding for UNFPA, have once again undermined U.S. leadership and influence with other donors.

■ **The U.S. administration and Congress need to reestablish a bipartisan commitment to UNFPA and increase the U.S. financial contribution to the Fund.** The U.S. contribution has fluctuated annually since 1993 and has not increased significantly since the early 1980s. An increased U.S. contribution to UNFPA is important to facilitate the flow of funds to countries which do not receive U.S. population assistance, especially as U.S. aid now goes to fewer countries. It would also reestablish U.S. credibility in the international population arena and increase its influence on multilateral population assistance programs.

Following the ICPD, UNFPA is positioned to significantly expand its influence on national policies and programs. It is a critical institution in the population field and one with greater potential than many other UN organizations. The Fund's leadership recognizes many of its weaknesses and is working to improve its effectiveness. Yet, for the Fund to be fully successful, the United States must recognize the role of the UN in addressing world population problems, and once again join the donor community in adequately supporting the work of UNFPA.

An increased U.S. contribution to UNFPA is important to facilitate the flow of funds to countries which do not receive U.S. population assistance.

1945 to 1995: The UN Contribution to the Population Field

I. The United Nations and World Population

Population has been one of the more effective areas of UN intervention.

During the first fifty years of the United Nations (UN), the world experienced two striking new demographic trends. As death rates declined sharply following postwar public health advances, population growth rates in developing countries rose to unprecedented levels. Between 1945 and 1995, the world's population more than doubled, from about 2.3 billion to 5.7 billion people.

Since the 1970s, however, population growth rates have slowed as average family size has declined dramatically in many countries. This decline reflects a growing preference for smaller families with social and economic progress, combined with the improved access to safe, effective contraception needed for couples to plan their families. However, desired family size in many countries remains above the two-child average needed to eventually stabilize population. The large proportion of young people yet to enter their childbearing years also provides enormous momentum for population growth in years to come.

The UN has been actively involved in population work since its early days. Concerned that mortality from war and disease could bring about a possible population decline, in 1946 UN leaders established the Population Division within the UN Secretariat to analyze demographic trends. UN researchers developed methodologies for demographic analysis and persuaded governments in developing countries to conduct the first round of national censuses.

When the findings from these early censuses became available in the early 1950s and 1960s, policymakers became concerned about rapid population growth and the UN's role expanded to include policy development and financial and technical assistance to population programs. Indeed, population has been one of the more effective areas of UN intervention — UN organizations have made critical contributions to both enhanced understanding of global population trends and to declines in mortality and fertility.

- Through improved demographic data collection and analysis, including projections of future population growth, the Statistical and Population Divisions in the UN Secretariat have helped bring rapid population growth to the attention of policymakers and stimulated the initiation of national population programs.
- The international population conferences, organized by the UN every 10 years since 1974, have helped build consensus within the world community on the importance of addressing population issues. They have also helped develop political support for national policies to promote sustainable population growth, and for voluntary family planning programs.
- The United Nations Population Fund (UNFPA) has helped expand access to safe, effective contraception for millions of women and men through the provision of funds, contraceptives and expert advice in over 160 countries.
- The World Health Organization (WHO) has been a leader in efforts to develop new and improved methods of contraception and in research on contraceptive safety, efficacy and acceptability. WHO has also provided worldwide technical leadership in adolescent and maternal health.
- The UN Children's Fund (UNICEF) has enhanced infant and child health around the world, especially through improved immunization coverage and management of diar-

Population Action International

rheal diseases. Both UNICEF and WHO have helped lower death rates and increase life expectancy worldwide.

The ICPD: Challenges and Emerging Needs

As the world approaches both a new century and a new millennium, the *Programme of Action* adopted at the International Conference on Population and Development (ICPD), held in Cairo in 1994, presents fresh challenges and opportunities for the population field. The ICPD was an important watershed; while the conference document reaffirms the importance of slowing population growth for social and economic development, it calls for a major shift in strategies to achieve this goal.

The consensus reached by 180 countries in Cairo substantially enlarges the scope of population programs. The Cairo action plan places family planning within a broader context of individual reproductive health. The plan calls for the expansion and improvement of family planning and other reproductive health services to meet still substantial unmet needs, while recognizing the significant progress of the past two decades. In addition, the plan emphasizes the empowerment of women through expanded access to education and economic opportunities, an agenda reinforced at the 1995 Fourth World Conference on Women in Beijing.

Many developing countries currently lack the funds, trained personnel and facilities needed to achieve the comprehensive ICPD vision of reproductive health and women's empowerment. The challenge for these countries is to adapt the ambitious goals agreed on in Cairo to local realities and to establish priorities for ICPD implementation. In addition, many low and middle income countries will need increased aid from donor countries to implement the plan of action.

These needs for donor assistance are varied and evolving. Many countries with well-established family planning programs now finance most program costs themselves and have substantial local expertise. However, these countries still often have a need for specialized technical advisory services. Meanwhile, poorer countries with fledgling programs and more limited local expertise need a broader range of external assistance. In sub-Saharan Africa, in particular, efforts to address rapid population growth and poor reproductive health status are just getting under way; resources are scarce and many countries will require donor assistance for some time to come. Thus, population assistance appears likely to remain a concern for the international community well into the next century.

The Case for Stronger UN Leadership in Population Assistance

Historically, technical and financial leadership in international population assistance has come from the United States. The U.S. Agency for International Development (USAID) has provided roughly half of total grant assistance to population programs over the past 30 years. Private U.S. agencies funded by USAID have provided technical leadership on all aspects of family planning program management to countries throughout the developing world.

American leadership, however, appears likely to decline in importance given the downward trend in U.S. development aid, including population assistance, and the reduced number of countries receiving U.S. support. This retrenchment, if it continues, is likely to result in significant gaps in population assistance. While

Countries' needs for donor assistance are varied and evolving.

some other donor countries are increasing their involvement, none currently has the capacity to replace USAID funds — or its hands-on style of technical assistance, which has proven so important to program effectiveness. On the eve of the 21st century, however, technical assistance efforts also need to place more emphasis on sustainability and on building national capacity.

There is a strong argument that global leadership on population issues would more appropriately come from an intergovernmental organization than a bilateral aid agency. Multilateral organizations such as the UN and the World Bank are politically neutral and able to provide long-term assistance to build local capacity. In contrast, bilateral donors often provide aid according to shifting political interests or lack sufficient resources and expertise to mount significant efforts.

The World Bank — the leading multilateral organization in economic development — has substantial potential to increase financing for population programs but is less well-equipped to offer technical expertise. The Bank's present *country*-centered structure and approach to setting program priorities, moreover, seriously limit its ability to exercise worldwide *sectoral* leadership. Its current involvement is also limited to the relatively small number of countries willing to finance population activities with borrowed funds rather than grant aid.

The UN, in many ways, is the most appropriate organization to take the lead role in addressing global population problems:

■ **The UN has more than 20 agencies or units working on population issues, including UNFPA, the largest and most influential UN organization in the population field.** UN agencies encompass a wealth of expertise and have the potential to provide technical assistance in a broad range of population related areas. UNFPA, which is the only multilateral organization to have population as its sole mandate, has more population staff than any other development agency.

■ **The UN has historically been an important channel for population assistance.** Over the past decade, the UN has accounted for about 30 percent of total international grant assistance to population programs — most of it channeled through UNFPA. As in other development sectors, the bulk of UN population funding (over 90 percent) comes from voluntary contributions designated specifically for population work by donor countries. In 1992 (the most recent year for which data are available) UN population expenditures amounted to $253 million — $204 million in voluntary contributions to UNFPA, just under $19 million from the UN's regular budget, and $30 million in voluntary contributions to four other UN agencies. In comparison, U.S. population assistance in that year was $326 million.

■ **The UN system has close to a universal presence with the largest network of country offices of any international development agency.** UNFPA provides population assistance to more countries than either USAID or the World Bank and is the only channel for such assistance to a number of countries. This underscores the potential for the UN — and especially UNFPA — to assume a greater leadership role in international population assistance.

■ **UNFPA was also the central player in building the consensus achieved in the ICPD *Programme of Action*.** Building on the leadership displayed in Cairo, the Fund in the eyes of many is the appropriate entity to carry forward the ICPD mandate and promote its implementation at the country level.

The UN is the most appropriate organization to take the lead in addressing global population problems.

Political and Financial Constraints on UN Leadership

Concerns about the effectiveness of the whole UN system, however, call into question the UN's ability to assume stronger leadership in population assistance. The UN, in general, has a poor reputation for administrative management. Critics regard the system as a bloated and inefficient bureaucracy often lacking in management and accountability. The responsibility, of course, largely lies with UN member states, who have failed to insist on management reform.

The main targets of external criticism have been the central UN Secretariat and the essentially independent specialized agencies — for example, WHO and the Food and Agriculture Organization (FAO). The various development and humanitarian funds and programs supported through voluntary contributions are widely considered to be better managed and more effective, including UNICEF, UNFPA, the World Food Programme, and the UN High Commissioner for Refugees.

Despite recent efforts to strengthen the role of the United Nations Development Programme (UNDP), the UN's development activities are fragmented and coordination is weak. The primary intergovernmental body charged with guiding the UN's social and economic development activities — the Economic and Social Council (ECOSOC) — is widely perceived to be ineffective. Multiple UN organizations make grants or maintain a presence at the country level, yet each of these organizations independently develops its own programs, although their work overlaps in multiple ways.

The UN has been slow to respond to these criticisms. Donor countries and critics have perceived efforts over the years to cut staff and improve efficiency as piecemeal and inadequate. With donor support for both the UN system and overall foreign aid declining, many UN agencies involved in development work are struggling to increase voluntary contributions. The decline in support has been most evident in the United States, where the Congress has cut funds for UN agencies more deeply than other foreign aid programs and is significantly in arrears in paying the assessed U.S. contributions to the regular UN budget and to the budgets of some other UN agencies.

The problem is less serious in Europe and Japan, where foreign office staff rather than politicians generally determine UN funding levels. But the United States is not alone. There is a broader retreat from internationalism and multilateralism. A few other donor countries have also cut their foreign aid programs, and many have long been clamoring for UN reform. These trends partly reflect the preoccupation in industrialized countries with internal economic problems, including budget deficits. But they also reflect the widespread perception that the UN as an institution — and as a channel for development assistance — is often less than optimally effective. The view that international trade is more successful than aid in promoting economic development has further undermined support for foreign aid, including population assistance.

Developing countries are more supportive of the UN. They see the UN as an important mechanism for correcting the imbalance in resources and power between rich and poor nations. While the rich industrialized countries value the UN primarily for its role in international peacekeeping, many poorer nations would like to see donor nations give development activities higher priority. In many developing countries, UN organizations have prestige and influence far exceeding

The UN's development activities are fragmented and coordination is weak.

the magnitude of funds they provide. Nevertheless, major changes are needed if the UN is to respond vigorously to the social and economic development needs of the 21st century — including implementation of the ICPD *Programme of Action*.

Objectives of PAI's Report

This report by Population Action International (PAI) focuses on the critical role of UNFPA, as the key UN organization in the population field, in helping countries apply the ICPD action program to their unique circumstances. It sets out steps that UNFPA can take to strengthen its leadership and programs, and that the rest of the UN system can take to better support UNFPA's efforts. It also highlights the importance of U.S. support for the UN's work in population.

Major sources for the report include interviews with experts and documents in the public domain. The report also draws extensively on two external evaluations of UNFPA, which involved visits to many of the Fund's field programs. These include a 1993 evaluation commissioned by the Canadian, Finnish and German international aid agencies and a 1995 review of UNFPA's technical support system prepared at the request of the Fund's Executive Board.

These official evaluations provide a comprehensive assessment of the operations of the Fund and its technical support system. The present report, however, focuses more narrowly on the most important policy and management challenges facing UNFPA as it seeks to respond to the needs in developing countries. At the same time, the report acknowledges the dynamic character of UNFPA. The Fund has already recognized and is attempting to address many of the issues identified in this report.

An effective UNFPA is critical for the long term well-being of the planet and its people and is an institution deserving of support. As the 1993 donor evaluation of UNFPA succinctly states, "UNFPA represents an important world-wide organization in the field of population. It fulfills a unique role, which cannot be replicated by other multilateral or bilateral agencies…the organization must be supported, strengthened and improved so that it can continue to address this mandate, but in a more effective way."

An effective UNFPA is critical for the long term well-being of the planet and its people.

II. UNFPA: Responding to the Needs of the 21st Century

The Importance of UNFPA in UN Population Activities

Despite the large number of UN organizations engaged in population work, only a few play a major role in population and reproductive health. As the principal funding agency, UNFPA stands out as the central actor within the system. The Population Division in the UN Secretariat, WHO and UNICEF also have important complementary but differentiated roles to play in helping developing countries meet the challenges that emerged from Cairo and Beijing.

The Population Division, primarily engaged in demographic research and analysis, is a resource for monitoring progress on key indicators relating to the ICPD agenda. WHO, with its medical and scientific expertise, is responsible for technical leadership in reproductive health. UNICEF has strong field programs and has recently given more emphasis to some aspects of reproductive health and to women's development, but has not given priority to family planning.

Other UN organizations, such as the International Labour Organization (ILO) and the UN Educational, Scientific and Cultural Organization (UNESCO), are not significantly involved in reproductive health, but have a role to play in supporting the broader linkages between population and development.

For the moment, this leaves UNFPA as the only UN organization directly assisting countries in mounting reproductive health and family planning programs. Through its financing of population work in other UN agencies, UNFPA is also well placed to promote greater synergy between population and development activities throughout the UN system. UNFPA is the critical institution in this area and is likely to grow in importance in the years to come.

UNFPA's Mission and Achievements

UNFPA was established in 1969, growing out of a UN Trust Fund for Population created two years earlier. At that time, a few donor countries saw a need for a UN organization focused solely on population and for a channel for funding population activities. A multilateral organization was perceived to have an advantage over government-to-government assistance in a politically and culturally sensitive area like population and family planning.

UNFPA is governed by an Executive Board comprising representatives of 36 UN member nations; it shares this Board, which reports to the UN Economic and Social Council and the General Assembly, with UNDP. While UNFPA has some freedom of action, it must take policy and administrative guidance from its Executive Board. Philosophical differences within the Board sometimes require lengthy and difficult negotiations. The northern European countries, which contribute the bulk of UNFPA's budget, have a strong influence on Board decisions.

UNFPA's mission was not formally articulated until 1973, when the Economic and Social Council approved the following objectives for the new agency:
- to *build capacity* to respond to needs in population and family planning;
- to *promote awareness* in both developed and developing countries of population problems and the human rights aspects of family planning, and of strategies to deal with them;
- to *assist developing countries* in dealing with population problems;
- to *play a leading role in the UN system* in promoting population programs and coordinating projects supported by the Fund.

As the principal population funding agency, UNFPA stands out as the central actor within the system.

Population Action International

Over the past 27 years, UNFPA has provided $3.4 billion in population assistance to 167 countries.

UNFPA has clearly accomplished a great deal towards fulfilling this mandate:

■ **UNFPA's most striking success has been in global advocacy.** Much credit goes to UNFPA's executive director, Dr. Nafis Sadik, and her predecessor, the late Rafael Salas, for using their position as a platform to make population issues less sensitive and to build international support for family planning programs. This strength was especially apparent in the success of the Cairo Conference, at which 180 nations agreed on the importance of addressing population growth and on the means to do so. UNFPA's skillful leadership in building bridges between diverse ideological views and encouraging participation by a wide array of nongovernmental organizations (NGOs) was key to the success of the ICPD process. UNFPA has also become an important voice for the social and economic advancement of women.

■ **UNFPA has been a significant source of grant assistance to developing countries for population activities.** Over the past 27 years, UNFPA has provided $3.4 billion in population assistance to 167 countries. UNFPA's program expenditures grew steadily in the 1970s. In the 1980s, expenditures fluctuated between $100 to $120 million a year for most of the decade. In the late 1980s, expenditures increased but dropped back again in 1992 and 1993. In 1995, UNFPA provided an all-time high of $231 million in project assistance — including unspent funds from the previous year — to about 150 countries.

■ **UNFPA continues to lead the UN system in ICPD follow-up and implementation.** The ICPD has been a major catalytic force, promoting increased dialogue and interaction within the UN system. Specialized agencies such as WHO, ILO, UNESCO, and FAO have made internal organizational changes to elevate population related activities as part of follow-up to the ICPD. The UN has regarded the interagency task force on ICPD implementation, led by UNFPA, as a model for follow-up of UN conference recommendations.

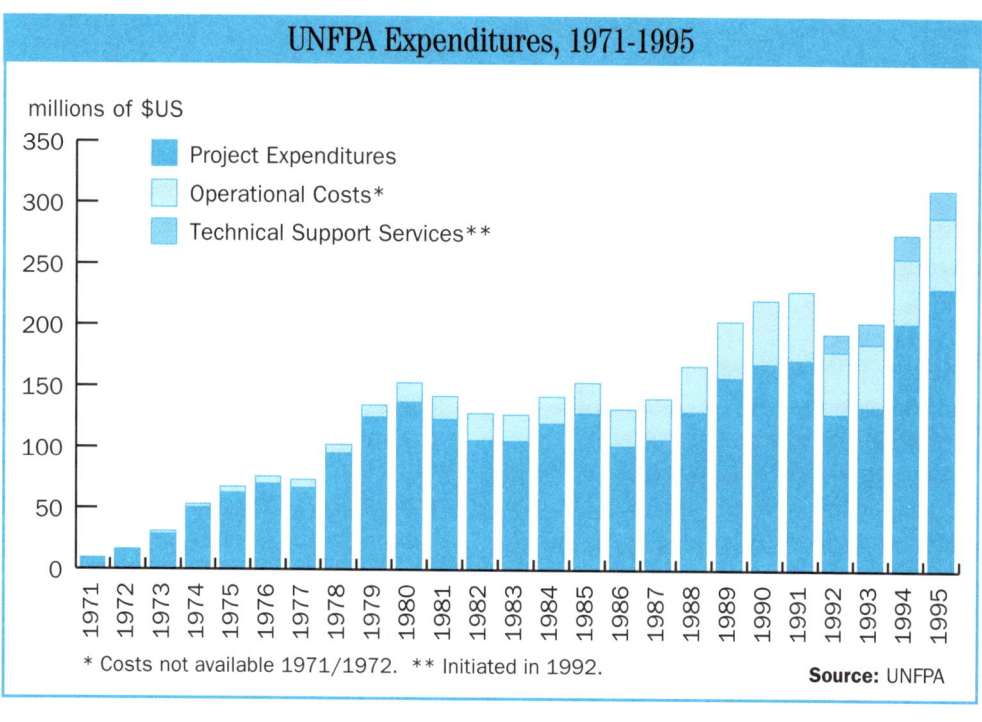

8   *Taking the Lead*

■ **In contrast with the reputation of much of the UN system, UNFPA is viewed as dynamic and evolutionary.** Its status as a voluntarily funded organization has enabled it to some degree to circumvent the UN bureaucracy. The Fund is widely considered to be better managed than most UN agencies. Working closely with its Executive Board, it has adapted its policies and programs to reflect major changes in the population field. UNFPA has also taken steps to improve program effectiveness and efficiency, sometimes at the cost of some loss of popularity with other UN agencies.

Extending UNFPA's Leadership from the Global to the Country Level

At the country level, however, the Fund's operational achievements have been mixed. In many countries, UNFPA has been an important source of advice and assistance. Overall, however, the Fund has not by any means fulfilled its potential for impact in either of its two key roles — in strategic leadership on national policy issues, or in technical and financial support to population programs.

Thus, UNFPA's principal challenge is to translate its success in global advocacy to operational success at the level of individual countries. There are several reasons why this is important. First, UNFPA may be the only donor agency with the potential to replace USAID's leadership in the population field. Second, roughly a third of total population aid is channeled through UNFPA; with needs exceeding available resources, it is important that UNFPA use available funds with maximum effectiveness and efficiency. Finally, as a major channel of assistance, UNFPA's ability to improve its impact at the country level is critical to satisfy donor nations that their funds are well spent and to increase the overall financial resources available to population programs.

The gap between UNFPA's potential and actual impact at the country level largely reflects the limitations of its funds and staff, relative to the number of countries requesting assistance and the scope of their needs. Although UNFPA can take a number of steps to strengthen its effectiveness, the shortfall in funding is real. The international community must recognize the importance of UNFPA and support the institution with adequate resources.

Challenges for the 21st Century

At its creation, UNFPA was intended to be a mechanism for raising donor funding for population projects developed by UN specialized agencies like WHO, UNESCO, ILO and FAO, thereby encouraging involvement of the broader UN system in population work. Over the years, however, in response to changing conditions and the mixed experience with the management of UNFPA-funded projects by other UN agencies, UNFPA and national governments have assumed a greater role in both technical and managerial oversight of project implementation. This shift away from project management by other UN agencies also reflects a UN-wide shift towards increased national execution and local capacity building.

Over the past decade, the share of UNFPA program funds channeled through other UN agencies has fallen dramatically, from 65 percent in 1984 to 15 percent in 1994. (This latter figure does not reflect funds which continue to flow to the specialized agencies under UNFPA's technical support system, described in more detail below.) In 1994, UNFPA managed over 40 percent of program funds,

At the country level, UNFPA's operational achievements have been mixed.

Over the past decade, the share of UNFPA program funds channeled through other UN agencies has fallen dramatically.

while national governments managed 24 percent.

As UNFPA looks to the future and seeks to support national implementation of the ICPD *Programme of Action*, it needs to further strengthen its effectiveness as an operational development agency. Moreover, the Fund must continue to respond dynamically to both changes in donor assistance and to the evolving needs in developing countries. This changing scene raises the following six critical challenges for UNFPA.

1. Increasing Global Funding for Population Programs

UNFPA has a lead role to play in raising the financial resources needed to implement the ICPD Programme of Action. The ICPD set ambitious funding goals based on the growing numbers of couples anticipated to have a need for family planning and other reproductive health services. To satisfy this anticipated demand, the ICPD estimated that reproductive health and family planning expenditures will need to reach $17 billion in constant 1993 dollars in the year 2000, and $22 billion in 2015. Of this amount, roughly $10 billion in 2000 and $14 billion in 2015 will be needed for family planning alone. The ICPD called for donor countries to provide one-third of overall population assistance — $5.7 billion by the year 2000.

No consistent data are yet available for current spending in developing countries on the improved and broadened package of reproductive health services recommended at the ICPD. However, current expenditures on family planning alone are estimated at about $4 to $5 billion. Donor contributions for population assistance amounted to approximately $1.2 billion in 1994. While this represents a significant increase, both donor and developing country expenditures clearly fall far short of the trajectory needed to reach ICPD spending goals.

Like UNICEF and UNDP, UNFPA is funded by voluntary contributions, as opposed to the fixed dues and assessments which finance the budgets of the UN secretariat and the UN system's specialized agencies. Historically, the UN has been an important channel for mobilizing population assistance — more than in other areas of development assistance. Donors like Denmark, Finland, Japan, the Netherlands and Norway — all of which have limited overseas staff and population expertise — have channeled almost all of their population assistance through multilateral institutions.

In 1995, a total of 85 countries contributed to UNFPA. Despite this broad base of support, a relatively small number of donor countries provide the bulk of UNFPA's resources. In 1995, UNFPA's largest donors, in descending order of the magnitude of funds provided, were Japan, the Netherlands, Denmark, the United States, Germany, Norway, Sweden, the United Kingdom and Finland.

The system of voluntary contributions has helped keep UNFPA more accountable and responsive to donors, and in turn has helped increase funding for UNFPA over time. Although contributions to UNFPA plateaued in the 1980s, they have increased steadily since the early 1990s, when the ICPD provided a stimulus to donor funding and the United States returned as a donor. UNFPA's prestige has also been significantly enhanced by the visibility and leadership demonstrated by the Fund's Executive Director, Dr. Sadik, during the Cairo process, and by management changes initiated in recent years.

Donor contributions increased to $261 million in 1994 and $293 million in 1995, and are expected to rise to

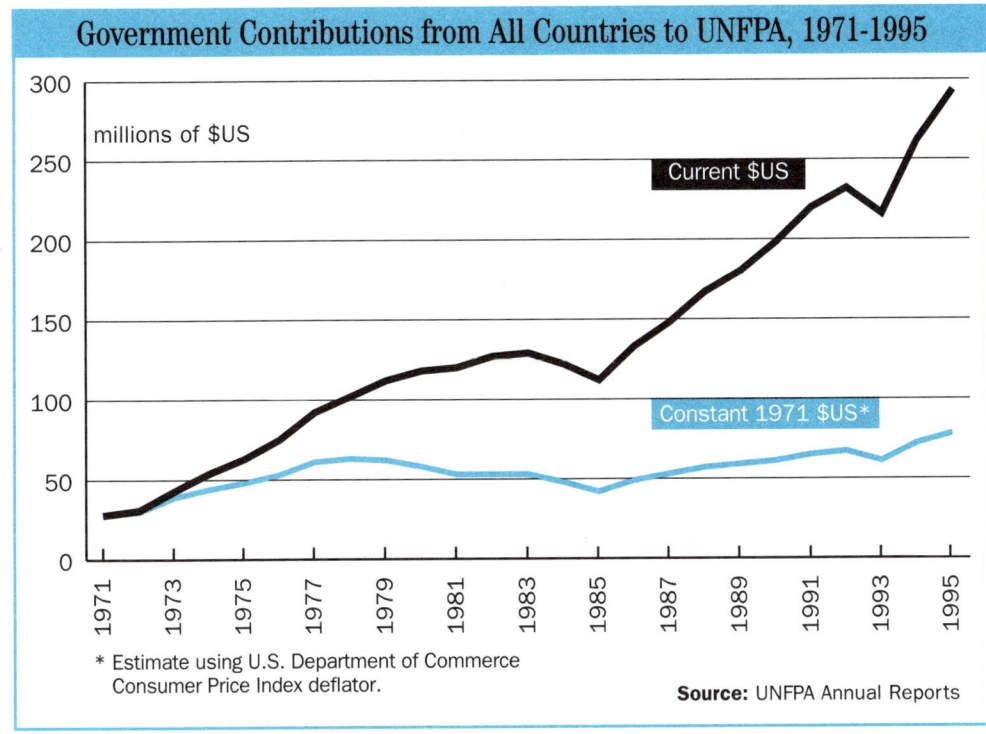

A major problem is the continuing lack of interest in population assistance shown by France, Italy and Spain.

over $300 million in 1996. Thus, UNFPA appears to enjoy a high degree of confidence among the major donor countries, at a time when many of them are reducing support to some UN specialized agencies.

Despite UNFPA's successes in global fundraising to date, many challenges remain with respect to the related goals of mobilizing funds for reproductive health and family planning programs in developing countries and increasing funds for UNFPA programs.

Uneven burden sharing among donor nations: The burden of overall population assistance remains uneven. A few donor countries — the United States, Germany, Japan, the United Kingdom, Norway, the Netherlands, Sweden and Denmark — currently contribute over 90 percent of all population assistance, and the bulk of UNFPA funds. Even among these countries, contributions differ substantially relative to their size and wealth. Norway, Denmark and the Netherlands have contributed the most on a per capita basis. The United States and Japan, two of the larger donors in absolute terms, have contributed less per capita.

A major problem is the continuing lack of interest in population assistance shown by European countries such as France, Italy and Spain. These countries — especially France — provide substantial foreign aid, but their population assistance remains negligible. Their contributions to UNFPA are also significantly lower than their contributions to such other UN funds as UNICEF and UNDP, totaling less than $3 million for the three countries in 1995.

Variable donor commitment to the UN channel: Within the donor community, commitment to multilateral assistance varies significantly. The Nordic countries and the Netherlands rely extensively on the UN to channel their contributions for development assistance, both because of a strong philosophical commitment to the UN system and because they have very limited technical and field personnel.

In some other countries, however,

Major Donor Country Contributions to UNFPA, 1993-1995

millions of $US

Legend: 1995, 1994, 1993

Countries (left to right): Japan, Netherlands, United States, Germany, Norway, Denmark, Sweden, United Kingdom, Canada, Finland, Switzerland, Belgium, Australia, Italy, France, Austria

Source: UNFPA Annual Reports 1993-1995

In recent years, the United States has been an unreliable source of funding for UNFPA.

a general lack of confidence in the UN system has limited multilateral population assistance. The German parliament has prohibited multilateral institutions from receiving more than 30 percent of total German aid in any sector. In the United Kingdom, decision-makers have channeled recent increases in population and reproductive health assistance largely through bilateral and NGO programs. Aid officials in these countries continue to support UNFPA, while expressing concern about the efficiency of the multilateral channel.

In recent years, the United States has been an unreliable source of funding for UNFPA. Formerly UNFPA's largest donor, the United States withheld its contribution to UNFPA from 1986 to 1992. In 1993, the United States restored its contribution to UNFPA, again becoming a major donor. In 1996, however, UNFPA once again became a prime target for congressional cuts in foreign aid and population assistance. Without a substantial U.S. contribution, some countries may limit their assistance on the grounds that contributions should reflect ability to pay.

Limited co-financing mechanisms: In a number of countries, UNFPA has helped mobilize additional funds by serving as a broker for bilateral donors, linking them with prospective developing country recipients. Under these multilateral-bilateral arrangements known as multi-bi, donors select the projects they wish to fund and either supplement UNFPA funds or provide grant funds directly. In 1994, multi-bi totaled about $17 million, equivalent to six percent of UNFPA expenditures. The major multi-bi donors have been Belgium, Canada, the Netherlands, Norway, Sweden, and the United Kingdom.

UNFPA's multi-bi mechanism has not been optimally effective. Because multi-bi funds have been tied to specific projects — usually small and with low policy leverage — the mechanism has limited flexibility and potential to raise significant additional donor contributions at the country level. The bureaucratic and lengthy process involved in joint programming with UN agencies, and the perception that financial controls and project supervision are lax in the UN system, have further deterred bilateral donors from pursuing multi-bi projects. In contrast, the World Bank has helped mobilize substantial bilateral grant funds to complement Bank credits in a number of countries, by taking the lead in developing large, highly leveraged programs for multi-donor funding.

Changing patterns of donor assistance: New channels for population assistance are emerging in a field traditionally dominated by USAID, UNFPA, and the World Bank. The British, German, and Japanese governments are expanding their bilateral programs. The European Union is moving to expand its role in population and reproductive health assistance. Developing countries with successful programs have joined together to create a new south-to-south partnership for technical cooperation. Regional development banks are also taking steps to become more involved in population programs.

The proliferation of channels of assistance suggests a need for greater coordination of donor assistance. UNFPA should be the lead external population adviser in a given country, helping the government coordinate donor assistance. Yet the 1993 evaluation points out that the Fund has played a variable and often informal role in facilitating donor coordination.

Thus, the growing pluralism in channels of population assistance represents a fluid funding environment that challenges UNFPA to demonstrate its usefulness. In the future, some of these new channels could potentially divert financial contributions from UNFPA, underscoring the need for the Fund to strengthen its effectiveness.

Inadequate resource mobilization efforts in developing countries: According to the ICPD *Programme of Action*, the bulk of the resources for population programs must come from developing countries themselves. To date, UNFPA has done relatively little to encourage developing country governments to increase their financial contributions. Such discussions, moreover, need to place reproductive health and family planning within the larger context of ongoing debates on health sector reform and financing in many developing countries, and to address the effective and efficient allocation of scarce public resources. A major drawback to advancing these discussions is the continuing lack of good national data on current expenditures on family planning; financial data on other reproductive health services are even harder to come by.

Weak monitoring of financial commitments: The international community has charged UNFPA with monitoring progress on ICPD implementation, including tracking financial commitments by both donor and developing countries. This is a complex task requiring the development

UNFPA should be lead external population adviser in a given country, helping the government coordinate donor assistance.

Profiles in UNFPA Assistance: Country Case Studies

TURKMENISTAN

Context of UNFPA Assistance: Turkmenistan — a former Soviet Republic — is one of UNFPA's smaller and newer programs. In mid-1996, UNFPA was the only donor in the population sector in Turkmenistan; UNICEF supports activities in the area of child health. In 1995, UNFPA allocated $705,742 for projects in Turkmenistan.

Field Office: The Fund's field office has two professional staff: a country representative and a national programme officer.

Program of Assistance: UNFPA's program, established relatively recently, supports two multi-year projects: a $2 million activity to strengthen the delivery of reproductive health services in the country; and a $726,000 information, education and communications (IEC) activity which supports the reproductive health services project.

UNFPA Partners: Both UNFPA assisted projects are with the Ministry of Health.

UNFPA should take on a more central role in identifying strategies for program financing.

of new definitions and monitoring systems to reflect the broader vision of population programs that emerged from the ICPD.

UNFPA has long made a major effort to track donor country commitments through its annual *Global Population Assistance Report*. However, the lead time for preparation of the report is too long. It also remains difficult to obtain reliable figures on population expenditures by the entire UN system. The Fund has made slower progress on developing new approaches to collecting data on expenditures by developing countries. In mid-1996, however, UNFPA solicited proposals from external institutions to advance the effort of tracking both donor and developing country expenditures on a more timely and complete basis.

Recommendation #1: UNFPA should further expand its efforts to raise global funding levels for population programs, as both an advocate and an expanded channel for donor assistance. UNFPA is the only organization that can advocate for enhanced levels of population funding with both the donor community and developing country governments. As a multilateral organization, it also remains the preferred channel for many traditional donors of population assistance, and one through which relative newcomers to the field can quickly expand their aid. It, therefore, serves multiple roles in mobilizing funding for population programs.

A key challenge for UNFPA is to persuade lagging donor countries to significantly increase their population assistance. The Fund must intensify ongoing direct advocacy efforts through its own staff, as well as indirect advocacy in cooperation with European groups to influence such donors as Italy, France, Belgium, Austria and Spain. The Fund must convince the leading donor countries in the field to seek to influence these more reluctant donors. Efforts to strengthen UNFPA's effectiveness are also essential if it is to increase the confidence and contributions of long-time donors in the population field.

UNFPA needs to do more at the national level to help countries secure the resources they need for their population programs. If UNFPA took on a more central role in identifying strategies for program financing, it could enhance its leverage independent of the size of its own country program. Beyond its own program, UNFPA could play an expanded role in helping developing countries identify program needs and generate requests to other donors for additional grant assistance for large-scale population programs.

By developing co-financing initiatives along the lines of the World Bank's donor consortia and encouraging donors to buy into programs rather than projects, UNFPA could help countries increase population assistance from bilateral and other donors. Close collaboration with Bank consultative groups and UNDP round tables could enhance the impact of these efforts, which in collaboration with others should extend beyond proposals for family planning and reproductive health programs to related activities such as girls education and women's development programs.

UNFPA needs to strengthen its advocacy aimed at increasing financial commitments for population and reproductive health programs from developing country governments. To accomplish this, it must form strategic alliances on a country by country basis with the World Bank, which has both significant expertise in broader health sector reform and financing issues and influence with ministries of finance.

In these efforts, the tracking of donor and national expenditures for reproductive health and family planning against ICPD funding goals remains a critical challenge. The Fund's initiative to contract out this function represents a sensible decision in light of staffing constraints at headquarters. However, the Fund needs to accelerate efforts to improve limited existing data on expenditures by developing country governments and consumers. This is a complex exercise requiring both quantitative and qualitative analysis of national public and private sector expenditures. UNFPA should consider establishing a special advisory group of outside experts to help guide its effort to gather comparable national data on population expenditures.

2. Enhancing Country Level Strategic Leadership: Becoming "Chief Population Advisor"

Following the ICPD, an important mandate for UNFPA is to help national governments reshape population policies and programs to implement the Programme of Action. In some respects, UNFPA is well suited to play this advisory role. As a UN organization, it is seen by developing countries as neutral and service oriented. The 1993 donor evaluation characterized UNFPA as a trusted adviser in the eyes of many governments. By all reports, UNFPA country representatives generally have excellent access to their government counterparts.

The Fund has helped move a number of African and Near Eastern governments towards developing population policies and programs, working behind the scenes in early policy development and laying the groundwork for other donors to help countries initiate large-scale family planning programs. The 1993 evaluation notes: "In many of the countries visited, the existence of a population policy, the creation of population units or councils and political awareness of the need to address population problems can be traced to UNFPA interventions at either the international or the country levels."

Nonetheless, there is a consensus that UNFPA needs to play a greater leadership role in the policy arena. Except in a few countries where it has been the only donor, the Fund is generally not perceived to have played a central role in providing governments with strategic policy advice regarding the development of national plans in population, reproductive health and family planning.

Several factors account for UNFPA's limited advisory role and influence on policy:

Marginalization in Policy Discussions: UNFPA country budgets are relatively small, constraining the Fund's influence with governments and other donors at the country level. The World Bank and USAID, which tend to take the lead on population policy matters, often provide substantially greater financial assistance. But there is also a general perception in the donor community that UNFPA has focused too narrowly on its own portfolio of projects rather than on the big picture. The tendency towards atomization of country portfolios into a large number of small projects, and the frequently peripheral nature of UNFPA projects to the main action of national programs, have also served to distance UNFPA from strategic discussions.

Stature of Country Representation: UNFPA's potential to provide leadership on policy issues is directly dependent on its country representatives. The 1993 donor evaluation commented: "One of the strengths of UNFPA has been the high quality of the Country Directors

UNFPA country budgets are relatively small, constraining UNFPA's influence with governments and other donors at the country level.

> *The caliber of individual country representatives is of crucial importance, given the limited staff in UNFPA field offices.*

(Representatives) who are very well trained, resourceful, and independent." Observers note that the quality of UNFPA representation at the country level has improved in the past three to four years. They cite Brazil, Ethiopia, Senegal, South Africa and Vietnam as instances where recently UNFPA has assumed a strong leadership role.

In the eyes of these same observers, however, there are as many instances where UNFPA has not shown sufficient leadership. The caliber of the individual country representatives is of crucial importance, given the limited staff in UNFPA field offices. Yet many of them lack the expertise and credibility to advise governments on complex population policy issues. The Fund also lacks the in-house expertise to support the full range of technical advice to governments, a constraint discussed at greater length below. To UNFPA's credit, it now recognizes that implementing ICPD requires country representatives to take the lead in initiating policy discussions. The Fund has indicated it will evaluate country representatives on their catalytic role in influencing policy and has begun to train them in advocacy.

Weak Research and Analytical Capability: Any efforts by UNFPA to provide strategic leadership and advice at the country level must be grounded in high quality analysis. Yet UNFPA's analytical work has been weak. The Program Review and Strategy Development (PRSD) reports, which guide UNFPA's work at the country level, vary in quality. Outside experts note they are often overly descriptive, diffuse, and short on data and critical analysis. Most documents lack adequate discussion relating to program financing. Other donors generally find the reports to be limited in utility and a poor basis for policy discussions, compared, for example, to sector memoranda prepared by the World Bank. Nevertheless, where there is limited donor interest in a country, the UNFPA reports often represent the only overview of the population sector.

Conservative Culture: Some donor country officials assert that, because of its close links to governments, UNFPA has not been sufficiently independent on policy issues requiring strong advocacy. Relative to its global leadership on issues such as sexuality education for adolescents and unsafe abortion, UNFPA has been less bold in raising these sensitive issues in policy discussions at the country level. However, this is slowly beginning to change following the ICPD.

UNFPA has also been slow to acknowledge the importance of the commercial sector and encourage innovations like contraceptive social marketing. Its efforts to influence policy have placed too much emphasis on the establishment and support of national population councils, which have a mixed record of effectiveness.

Recommendation #2: UNFPA needs to play more of an advocacy and policy role in implementing the ICPD accords, working more closely with the World Bank. The ICPD document represents UNFPA's mandate at the country level. UNFPA representatives need to work with governments, other UN agencies, NGOs and other donors to help countries create their own ICPD plan of action. Within the UN system, UNFPA country representatives should also work closely with the UN resident coordinators, who head the UN presence in country and have access to political leaders and policymakers in other sectors.

To successfully assume this role, UNFPA country representatives must be able to provide sound and credible policy advice. UNFPA's leadership and Executive Board need to ensure that country representatives have the stature and policy expertise to advise a country's top leadership. At the same time, UNFPA must develop the support systems to free country representatives from mundane reporting work and help them refocus on policy discussions.

In this enhanced role, UNFPA should do more to help countries plan the expansion and improvement of reproductive health and family planning services beyond its own financial and technical assistance to these efforts. It could also take the lead in helping countries develop plans to expand related programs such as education for girls and economic opportunities for women with funding from other sources. If UNFPA had stronger capacity for high quality policy analysis and program design work, it is likely that a number of other donors — including the World Bank — would follow its lead. In some countries, however, individual personalities or the relative size of donor programs may militate against other donors accepting a larger role for UNFPA.

UNFPA needs to support efforts to exert greater intellectual leadership and to influence policy with stronger technical and analytical work. UNFPA must begin by strengthening its own capacity for sound analysis of national policies and programs. However, UNFPA could also draw more on the staff of the UN Population Division, with its reputation for intellectual excellence, to bring increased rigor to its in-country analytical work. UNFPA could similarly strengthen its relationships with private groups such as the Population Council to get help in these areas.

Joint sector reviews with the World Bank could also help to increase UNFPA's engagement in policy discussions as well as to improve the design and quality of UNFPA-funded programs. Effective models for collaboration between UN agencies and the Bank already exist in the water supply sector. One practical problem with joint analytical work in the population field is that the Bank does not carry out sector work in every country. The principle is that wherever possible UNFPA should seek to build on the work of other donors and organizations with stronger analytical capability.

To increase its influence at the policy level, UNFPA needs to strengthen its working relationships with the World Bank more generally, both with the country departments at headquarters and with the resident missions. The Bank's comparative advantage lies in its strong policy leadership, close relationship with governments, and access to ministers of finance and heads of state. As such, it represents a potentially important vehicle to incorporate

---

Profiles in UNFPA Assistance: Country Case Studies

EGYPT

Context of UNFPA Assistance: UNFPA is the second largest donor in the population sector in Egypt, allocating approximately $3.5 million in 1995. USAID is by far the largest donor, providing over $15 million in 1995. The European Union, Germany, IPPF and the Netherlands each contribute between $500,000 and $1.5 million in population assistance annually.

Field Office: The UNFPA has four professional staff in Egypt, including a country representative, international programme officer, and two national programme officers. The office also has six other clerical and support staff.

Program of Assistance: In mid-1996, UNFPA's program supported 17 projects. The largest is a $1.7 million, four-year effort to strengthen the National Population Council; the smallest, a $235,000 four-year project to train nurses in Assiut Governorate in family planning counseling. The UNFPA portfolio in Egypt has a strong emphasis on population education and includes activities directed at workers, school children, out of school youth, university staff and students, as well as agricultural extension efforts. The Fund also supports family planning service delivery through several NGOs, and it supplies injectable contraceptives to the government health and family planning program. In addition, three projects aim to strengthen national capacity in population research and analysis. Finally, UNFPA supports a national NGO committee which aims to help NGOs in their efforts to implement the ICPD plan of action.

UNFPA Partners: Implementing agencies for these projects include the Ministries of Health and Education, the National Population Council, the UN Food and Agriculture Organization (FAO), national statistical institutions, and several NGOs.

If UNFPA had stronger capacity for high quality policy analysis, it is likely that other donors would follow its lead.

UNFPA's 1995 worldwide program budget of $289 million was divided among more than 150 countries.

population issues in discussions on macroeconomic policy and to increase the priority given to population programs by top national leaders.

Where UNFPA plays an important advocacy and advisory role, country offices may have higher administrative costs relative to program funding. UNFPA's leadership and Executive Board need to recognize and accept the potential for higher administrative costs associated with effective performance of these critically important and highly leveraged functions.

3. Thinking Big: Increasing the Impact of UNFPA Country Programs

With an annual budget representing roughly a third of global population assistance, UNFPA is an important source of financial support for efforts by national governments to implement the ICPD Programme of Action. Following the ICPD, UNFPA has taken a number of steps aimed at strengthening the effectiveness and impact of its assistance. These include development of new criteria for the allocation of its financial resources and redefinition of core areas of program activity.

Nevertheless, UNFPA faces a number of challenges in its efforts to allocate resources for maximum impact. As a multilateral organization, UNFPA cannot play favorites with different countries and is expected by UN member states to respond to requests for assistance, even when other donor funding is available. Resource allocation issues remain controversial within the Fund's Executive Board; Latin American and Eastern European countries on the Board have reportedly been unhappy with the Fund's emphasis on Africa. Despite the previous system of priority countries, UNFPA has followed the principle that no developing country seeking UNFPA's help will be denied assistance. These tensions have limited UNFPA's ability to deploy its resources strategically.

UNFPA funds have been spread too thin across too many countries, and, within countries, already limited resources have been splintered across too many program areas and too many small projects.

Too Many Countries: Recognizing the importance of action at the national level, UNFPA has consistently devoted the bulk of its financial resources to country programs. In recent years, the Fund has allocated about 80 percent of program expenditures to country-level activities and 20 percent to regional and worldwide programs.

UNFPA's 1995 worldwide program budget of $289 million was divided among more than 150 countries. Because UNFPA works in so many countries, the level of program resources available in most countries remains very limited. Despite efforts to develop sound criteria for allocating funds, this fragmentation of resources has significantly limited the impact of country programs.

The average annual country allocation for 1995 was about $1.8 million; the median allocation was about $0.9 million. Some 81 UNFPA country programs had budgets of less than $1 million. Of 154 countries assisted by UNFPA in 1995, 14 had annual UNFPA inputs of $5 million or more. This analysis supports the statement by the 1993 donor evaluation that, "The number of countries…UNFPA is trying to serve exceeds its organizational and financial capacity."

In the past, in its efforts to balance considerations of universality and program impact, UNFPA designated priority countries deserving a greater share of overall funding. Criteria for selection emphasized demographic factors and the need for international assistance, resulting in a strong focus on sub-Saharan Africa. In recent

Distribution of UNFPA Programs by Budget Size, 1994 & 1995

Program Budget ($US)	Number of Countries 1994	Number of Countries 1995
Under $1 million	84	81
$1 - 2 million	36	28
$2 - 3 million	9	18
$3 - 4 million	8	12
$4 - 5 million	6	1
over $5 million	8	14

Budgets over $5 million:

1994		1995	
Indonesia	$ 5,256,619	Nepal	$ 5,148,836
Kenya	$ 5,705,209	Morocco	$ 5,173,122
Ethiopia	$ 6,646,136	Uganda	$ 5,240,104
Nigeria	$ 7,016,955	Yemen	$ 5,350,007
Bangladesh	$ 7,211,001	Kenya	$ 6,285,479
China	$ 7,241,153	Tanzania	$ 6,709,006
Vietnam	$ 10,694,064	Pakistan	$ 7,094,326
India	$ 15,089,115	China	$ 8,063,516
		Vietnam	$ 8,779,165
		Nigeria	$ 9,182,938
		Ethiopia	$ 9,433,667
		Philippines	$ 9,584,174
		Bangladesh	$ 10,566,805
		India	$ 15,471,138

Source: UNFPA Annual Reports 1994 & 1995

UNFPA has played a more critical role in countries where few other major donors provide population assistance.

years, UNFPA has allocated about 70 percent of funds for country programs to roughly 60 priority countries.

Following the ICPD, UNFPA has revised criteria for resource allocation. Financial assistance will now focus on countries with the lowest achievement in meeting ICPD goals relating to access to reproductive health and family planning services and education for girls, and with high infant and maternal mortality. UNFPA proposes to limit or phase out financial assistance to countries that have achieved or are close to achieving ICPD goals. However, it will continue to furnish technical assistance to any country that requests it. Countries in transition such as those in Eastern Europe and the former Soviet Union would also be eligible for temporary financial assistance.

UNFPA has limited experience with this new system for resource allocation. Analyses of the new system, however, suggest it will modestly improve but not solve the problem of dispersion of resources. Sixty countries fall in the neediest category; the share of program resources allocated to these countries is expected to increase significantly, from 51 percent at present to 65 to 69 percent. The remaining 30 to 35 percent of UNFPA resources will be shared among another 51 countries.

The importance of UNFPA resources at the country level — relative to other sources of funds — varies greatly. In general, UNFPA has played a more critical role in countries where few other major donors provide population assistance. These include Cambodia, Iran, Laos, Vietnam and a number of small African countries. In 37 of 140 countries receiving

Implications of New UNFPA Resource Allocation Criteria

Countries Grouped by Need for Population Assistance	Number of Countries	Share of Total Population (1995) %	Share of Resources	
			Current %	Proposed %
Group A (High Need)	60	45	51	65-69
Group B (Moderate Need)	39	24	35	22-24
Group C (Limited Need)	12	31	11	5-7
All Groups	111	100	100*	100*

*Includes negligible funding for other countries not included in this table.

Reproduced from: UNFPA. "A Revised Approach for the Allocation of UNFPA Resources to Country Programmes." DP/FPA/1996/15 February 5, 1996. New York: UNFPA, 1996.

UNFPA-funded programs have lacked a strong strategic focus.

UNFPA assistance at the time of the 1993 donor evaluation, the Fund provided more than two-thirds of total population assistance. In contrast, UNFPA's assistance has been dwarfed by other donors in Indonesia and Bangladesh, where UNFPA has had large programs but where its assistance has represented only a very small share of overall program funds.

Too Many Program Areas and Small Projects: In the aftermath of the ICPD, UNFPA has recognized the need for new program directions and is making an effort to bring about changes. In doing so, an important challenge for UNFPA is to bring greater coherence to its assistance in individual countries.

UNFPA supports many good projects. However, there is a consensus in the international population community that UNFPA-funded programs have lacked a strong strategic focus, and that in many countries, UNFPA has not identified an appropriate niche for its assistance. As a result, country allocations — often small to begin with — have been spread across too many program areas.

The weakness of UNFPA's analytical work, discussed above, has been a further impediment to the identification of critical program areas where the Fund has the potential to make a difference. UNFPA workplans and projects have often been developed without reference to a larger, coherent program framework. In general, the Executive Board has not subjected the content of country assistance programs to close review.

Until recently, UNFPA had five workplan categories or program areas. UNFPA-funding for country programs has followed a pattern of including activities from each area. Critics note that UNFPA assistance to countries has taken a cookie-cutter approach, developing similar projects for each workplan category across countries, without sufficient local input. UNFPA's earlier system of dividing its funds among various UN agencies also contributed to the proliferation of program areas.

Over time, the emphasis of UNFPA programs has shifted from supporting demographic research and data collection to maternal-child health and family planning services. In recent years the latter has typically been the most important workplan category in most countries, receiving on average about half of country program funds. Nevertheless, the 1993 evaluation found that UNFPA's broad mandate had contributed to the lack of coherence of the Fund's programs, resulting in "…dilution of effort. It is simply not possible, given the limited amount of available resources, to adequately handle all aspects of the population problem at the same time."

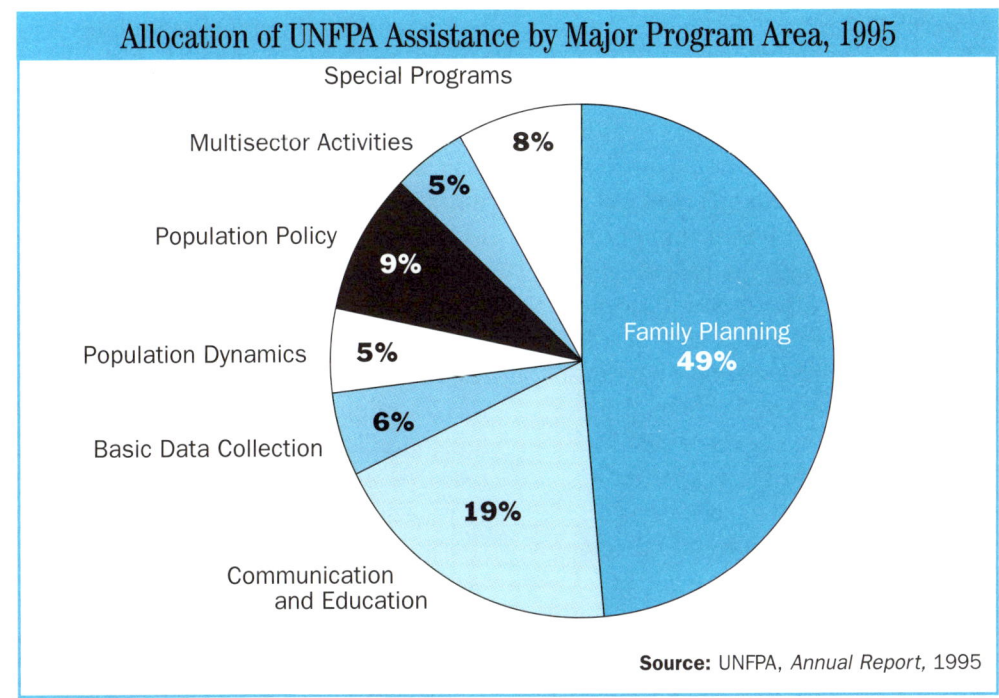

> "UNFPA thinks too small" is a frequent refrain among experts familiar with UNFPA's programs.

UNFPA also funds a very large number of small projects. "UNFPA thinks too small" is a frequent refrain among experts familiar with the Fund's country programs. UNFPA's 1995 annual report shows a program budget of $289 million and 2,479 projects. (The actual number of projects may be somewhat smaller since many projects listed in UNFPA's information system apparently represent one of two or three major budget components within a larger project.) This atomization of country portfolios has been detrimental to program impact and integration, while increasing the management burden on UNFPA staff.

Constraints to Program Effectiveness: A number of other factors have further undermined the effectiveness of UNFPA programs. UNFPA assistance has generally favored government programs over the more dynamic private sector. While UNFPA has supported NGO activities in many countries, this support has rarely been a major thrust of its country portfolios. Although UNFPA and the International Planned Parenthood Federation (IPPF) have cordial relations, there is surprisingly little collaboration between UNFPA and national IPPF affiliates. In most countries, UNFPA has not worked with the commercial sector and contraceptive social marketing. In some cases, this reflects an explicit effort to coordinate with other donors such as USAID, which provide assistance in these areas.

UNFPA faces some political difficulties in funding the private sector, since governments often want to reserve funds from multilateral donors for public sector programs. However, UNFPA's lack of support for the private sector has also been the outcome of an organizational culture lacking in innovation. With a strong mandate from the ICPD document, the Fund is now seeking to expand partnerships with international and national NGOs. It is also reportedly drafting new guidelines for working with the private sector — a development that is long overdue.

Evaluation has been a further weakness. Many projects are relatively small and of short duration and do not lend themselves to rigorous evaluation. UNFPA has not built

There are promising signs of change in UNFPA's overall program and culture.

quantitative indicators for evaluation into its programs. The fragmented nature of UNFPA's country portfolios has also made it difficult to evaluate country programs. Thus, while UNFPA has detailed information describing the activities it supports, it often has difficulty demonstrating the importance and purpose of its country programs. UNFPA's lack of a firm grasp of the impact of its programs undermines the confidence of donors, who want to see concrete results.

New Program Directions: Recognizing these weaknesses, in April 1995, UNFPA adopted three new program areas to facilitate ICPD implementation: *reproductive health and family planning; population policy*; and *advocacy*. In her report to the Board, Executive Director Dr. Sadik states: "The selection of these three areas will enable UNFPA to sharpen the strategic focus of its programming…It will also allow the Fund to pursue a holistic approach in addressing the specific population needs of individual countries."

■ *Reproductive health and family planning* is expected to be a central element of UNFPA assistance. UNFPA plans to continue to give priority to family planning, while incrementally broadening its assistance to support other reproductive health activities at the primary care level.

■ Under the *population policy* component, UNFPA will continue to help countries in the formulation of population policies. It will continue to provide some assistance for demographic data collection and analysis and for research on linkages between population and development, while reducing support to censuses and vital registration systems.

■ Although UNFPA has long experience as an advocate for population programs, establishment of *advocacy* as a distinct program area is a major departure from the past. UNFPA's advocacy activities will stimulate awareness of population and family planning issues and the importance of related social goals like girls' education and women's empowerment, with the aim of moving governments to implement the ICPD plan of action.

Thus, UNFPA has made some significant changes, although it is too early to judge results. It appears to be moving strongly in the direction of the broader reproductive health approach agreed on at the ICPD and towards greater innovation. Profiles of recently approved projects indicate that in Nigeria, UNFPA and UNICEF are collaborating on a mass media campaign on reproductive health. UNFPA now supports HIV/AIDS prevention activities in 103 countries. Some of these activities also address the prevention of other sexually transmitted diseases and include educational programs aimed at men.

The 1995 report also shows a significant increase in the number of countries with program budgets of $5 million or more, and a reduction in the total number of projects. Although some projects remain relatively small, the trend appears to be towards larger projects. These are all promising signs of change in the Fund's overall program and culture.

Recommendation #3: UNFPA needs to be more focused and strategic in selecting countries and program areas. The revised parameters for resource allocation do not alleviate the fundamental scarcity of resources. Neither the new criteria nor the new program themes represent an instant solution to the problems of dispersion of resources and limited impact.

To this end, UNFPA must work with its Executive Board to further refine its paradigm for resource allocation. UNFPA cannot have a real impact in 60 priority countries with the staff and financial resources it can reasonably anticipate having over the near term. It needs to establish criteria that will allow it to choose a smaller, manageable number of countries in which to make serious investments of staff and funds. While politically difficult, this strategy could greatly magnify the impact of the Fund's country programs.

Selection of countries should be based on the resources and skills available to UNFPA, the needs of the countries themselves, and an assessment that UNFPA can play a crucial role in the country. The ICPD document remains the blueprint for action, and the indicators of need relating to ICPD goals, which UNFPA has developed as a guide to resource allocation, remain relevant. However, the Fund needs to give more weight to such factors as absorptive capacity for assistance, the availability of other donor assistance, and the complementarity between the activities of other donors and UNFPA's capacities — both in terms of program areas and policy and technical advice.

As the only population donor with a universal mandate, it may prove difficult for UNFPA to withdraw entirely from countries. It could, however, designate certain countries as "minimum presence" countries where it would not make major commitments of staff or funds. For example, in countries where UNFPA assistance represents a small share of total program funds, UNFPA could cut back to a very limited profile aimed at monitoring program developments. The Fund could make periodic visits to hold discussions with the government, or perhaps even make a small grant to a local NGO to maintain a foothold in the country, performing these roles from offices in neighboring countries.

The Executive Board and the Fund need to remain flexible in identifying countries for the investment of financial and staff resources. There may be opportunities for the Fund to play a key strategic or coordinating role, or to fill critical gaps in assistance, even in some countries where its financial contribution is relatively small.

Within countries, UNFPA needs to establish strategic priorities at the country level, focusing on program areas that will move the population sector forward. UNFPA should identify specific roles in each country tailored to the local context. The new program categories are even broader than the old and could justify support for virtually any activity. Thus, as UNFPA develops new country assistance programs, it needs to review them closely and ensure they meet standards for greater focus and impact. To accomplish this, it will have to overhaul its programming procedures and work with govern-

---

Profiles in UNFPA Assistance: Country Case Studies

VIETNAM

Context of UNFPA Assistance: In 1995, the Fund allocated $8.8 million for projects in Vietnam, one of its larger programs. As the largest single donor in the population field, UNFPA has played a leadership role in Vietnam. Australia, Sweden and Germany also provide substantial bilateral population assistance, while France and Belgium provide modest assistance through UNFPA multi-bilateral programs.

Field Office: The UNFPA office has six professional staff, including a country representative, one international and three national programme officers, and a junior professional officer; and five support staff.

Program of Assistance: UNFPA funds 26 active projects. By far the largest activities support the provision of contraceptives, family planning equipment and drugs, and expert assistance in logistics to the Ministry of Health (roughly $15 million over two to three years). Other projects support contraceptive social marketing; quality control for local production of condoms; training of health workers in maternal health and family planning; and the National Committee for Population and Family Planning. A number of the Fund's projects also seek to improve data collection and analysis through support for census activities, demographic surveys, civil registration systems, computer and statistical training, and a population information center. UNFPA also funds educational outreach programs through diverse national organizations; a national IEC program; training on population for mass media workers; and population education in the formal school system.

UNFPA Partners: UNFPA provides assistance to the National Committee for Population and Family Planning and five government ministries, including the Ministry of Health. It also works with the national statistical office; the national women's, youth, farm and labor organizations; a university; and a condom factory.

UNFPA cannot have a real impact in 60 priority countries with its current staff and financial resources.

ments to create more synergistic and coherent programs of assistance, as opposed to an agglomeration of small projects. As part of efforts to be more strategic, it should also lift its sights upwards and develop "fewer, larger, higher quality projects with potentially stronger impacts."

UNFPA needs to further operationalize its new program themes. The themes of reproductive health and population policy build on UNFPA's previous work. The concept of advocacy is new, however. While it makes sense in a context where UNFPA has limited funds and expertise and yet seeks to promote a broader population and development agenda than in the past, UNFPA's specific plans for this area need further elaboration and sharpening.

In its efforts to establish strategic priorities and enhance the effectiveness of its programs, UNFPA must be more open to working with the private sector. UNFPA needs to channel more money through voluntary agencies and be more proactive and risk-taking in its support to activities such as contraceptive social marketing and efforts to involve private physicians.

Finally, UNFPA needs to develop a more results oriented culture and carry out more impact evaluations. A high priority should be to strengthen the Fund's in-house capability in evaluation and program related research. Program and project plans should include measurable objectives and appropriate monitoring and evaluation activities including data collection. UNFPA also needs to shift the emphasis of evaluation efforts from the project to the country program level. Enhanced program evaluation and feedback are crucial to making programs more effective, and improved evidence of impact remains the best prescription to boost donor confidence in and contributions to UNFPA.

4. Meeting the Technical Assistance Needs of the 21st Century

A key role for UNFPA, in supporting implementation of the ICPD Programme of Action, is to build in-country technical capacity, especially in the area of reproductive health and family planning. UNFPA needs to be able to provide technical assistance in all critical aspects relating to the implementation of reproductive health programs — for example, service delivery, human resources planning, program financing, evaluation, and procurement and logistics.

The likelihood that USAID-funded technical assistance will be less available and other donors will be unable or reluctant to provide expert assistance suggests UNFPA will grow in importance as a source of technical expertise. UNFPA is also a logical source of technical assistance because this support is on grant terms; most aid-recipient countries prefer to spend grant funds, rather than World Bank loans, to pay for technical advisers. As a multilateral organization, UNFPA is also well situated to promote the use of emerging developing country expertise. It has recently initiated support to the new south-to-south partnership, launched by 10 developing countries at the ICPD, for the provision of technical assistance in the population field.

Over the past five years, UNFPA has restructured and strengthened its technical support arrangements, but current arrangements do not go far enough towards meeting the needs of developing countries for state-of-the-art expertise. The Fund's role in technical assistance has been constrained by two factors: first, its limited internal technical capacity both at its New York headquarters and in its field offices; and second, its continuing reliance for technical services on other UN agencies lacking a depth of specialized population and

> *UNFPA is likely to grow in importance as a source of technical expertise.*

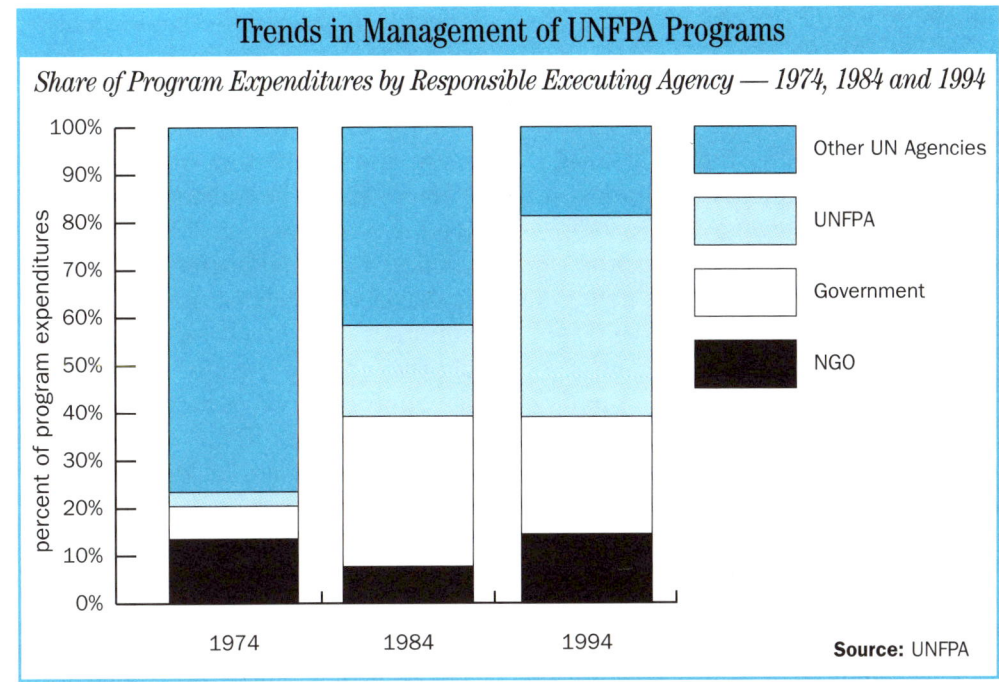

UNFPA has a long and mixed history of project execution by UN specialized agencies.

family planning expertise. Since internal staffing issues are discussed in a subsequent section, the focus here will be on UNFPA's arrangements for the provision of external technical expertise.

As noted earlier, UNFPA has a long and mixed history of project execution by UN specialized agencies. For over 20 years, UNFPA provided funds to these agencies to implement population projects. These agencies employed long-term advisers and short-term consultants at the headquarter, regional and country levels to oversee UNFPA-funded projects. However, these agencies, lacking a base of specialized, institutional expertise, often did not appoint the right types of advisers. As a result, technical services were frequently of poor quality and lacking in timeliness. UNFPA also experienced continuing problems with financial accountability by the agencies.

In light of this experience, UNFPA drastically revised the role of other UN agencies in providing technical support for UNFPA-funded projects. In 1991, UNFPA instituted a new Technical Support System (TSS), which brought together experts from different UN agencies in multidisciplinary teams that directly backstop UNFPA country programs. Each country support team includes a combination of public health, demographic, policy, communication and other experts, with the aim of providing coordinated advice to countries.

The teams operate out of eight regional offices close to the countries they support. They work at the request of countries and UNFPA representatives, and are available for activities other than tasks related to specific UNFPA projects. The regional development banks and the Netherlands are among other donors who have used this service.

In 1994 to 1995, the system included 122 experts on eight country teams and 42 specialists at agency headquarters who provided technical support to personnel on the country teams. Team members have been recruited primarily from the ranks of UN specialized agencies, although UNFPA has recruited some experts through NGOs and direct appointments. Team

The new technical support system represents an innovative mechanism that is still evolving.

members have two-year contracts, providing for the mix of skills to change in response to program needs.

A recent evaluation found the new technical support system to be a significant improvement, contributing to better project design and more effective and timely technical backstopping of UNFPA projects. The new system has filled an important need, as UNFPA has delegated increasing authority to its thinly staffed country offices, which together with national governments have gradually taken over considerably more responsibility for project execution from the specialized agencies. The new system has also reduced UNFPA's financial support and overhead payments to the specialized agencies, while increasing accountability. Within the UN system, the scheme represents an innovative mechanism that is still evolving.

Lack of appropriate expertise: At the same time, the evaluation identified a number of problems. The mix of advisers has not always reflected program needs. Most notably, at the time of the evaluation there was a critical shortage of advisers in the key area of maternal-child health and family planning, which has represented roughly half of UNFPA program funding. Vacancies for advisers in this area were attributed in large part to a lack of responsiveness and prompt recruitment of staff by WHO, which has primary responsibility for deploying advisers in these areas. The evaluation also perceived the number of experts at agency headquarters to be excessive, given the limited support they provided to the country teams.

In other ways too, the system has not been responsive to existing needs. Many countries with mature programs would like to use the system as a way of contracting outside technical specialists with leading edge skills, but do not perceive the teams to have this caliber of expertise. "Most of the demands in Asia are for sophisticated state-of-the-art backstopping, in many cases calling for niche expertise not available in the TSS system. In this regard, the TSS system is perceived as somewhat of an impediment to meeting such demands." The evaluation noted that the teams have emphasized project formulation and support, rather than broader analytical tasks and the transfer to developing country counterparts of state-of-the-art expertise.

At the same time, TSS staff have been unable to provide countries with nascent programs, especially in Africa, with the continuous support they need. Thus, although less advanced countries have heavily utilized the teams, the brevity and infrequency of their missions have impeded local capacity-building. In the words of a donor official, "UNFPA's technical support arrangements remain weak."

Inadequate reliance on private sector expertise: A major weakness of the present technical support system is that it does not take sufficient advantage of expertise outside the UN system, especially the wealth of NGO and other private-sector expertise. For example, private U.S. organizations supported by USAID have been the driving force behind the scientific management of population and family planning programs in the developing world. A substantial base of local expertise is also now emerging in a growing number of developing nations, and in some other donor countries.

At the country level, UNFPA has often forged creative and effective partnerships with these groups. In India, for example, UNFPA has funded AVSC International to help develop "centres of excellence" aimed at improving the quality of clinical contraceptive services. In Pakistan, where USAID has withdrawn population assistance, UNFPA is supporting service delivery and technical assistance activities in collaboration with several U.S. and national NGOs.

Such innovation depends largely on the initiative of individual UNFPA country representatives. UNFPA currently lacks global or regional mechanisms to help national governments and UNFPA country offices easily tap into private international expertise from outside the UN system. UNFPA's central funding for NGO programs has focused on research and information exchange rather than technical services to operational programs, in line with the perception that the country teams have primary responsibility for technical support. In some instances where other UN agencies have been unable to provide appropriate expertise, however, UNFPA has staffed some of the country team positions through NGO contracts. This trend should be encouraged to attract the highest quality professionals.

Recommendation #4: UNFPA needs to expand partnerships outside the UN system if it is to become the primary source of high quality technical expertise.

In the short-term, UNFPA needs to strengthen the existing technical support system. It should move some experts from headquarters to the field and intensify oversight to ensure the timely recruitment of high quality, relevant expertise and the removal of those who do not make the grade.

UNFPA should also reexamine the regional team approach and consider assigning these resources to UNFPA country offices. If all the advisers in the current system were divided among countries classified by UNFPA as having the greatest need, field offices in those countries could add an average of three international professional staff, significantly strengthening their managerial and technical capacity.

In looking to the future, UNFPA should move towards a system where international NGOs and other private sector groups can compete for global or regional technical assistance contracts. Especially in reproductive health and family planning, UNFPA is likely to find more effective partnerships among specialized private organizations than among UN agencies, with the possible exception of WHO and UNICEF. It should be much more proactive in diversifying its sources of technical assistance.

At the same time, UNFPA needs to encourage the development of NGO and other private sector expertise in developing countries. In its efforts to explore new ways to obtain technical services from outside the UN system, UNFPA should emphasize transfer of

A major weakness of the present technical support system is that it does not take sufficient advantage of expertise outside the UN system.

Profiles in UNFPA Assistance: Country Case Studies

TANZANIA

Context of UNFPA Assistance: UNFPA's assistance to Tanzania is substantial; the Fund allocated $6.7 million for projects in Tanzania in 1995. The United States has been the largest single source of population assistance to Tanzania, providing over $9 million in 1995. Germany and Britain are other major donors, while the European Union, Norway and the Netherlands also provide assistance in reproductive health.

Field Office: UNFPA's professional staff of five include a country representative, one international and two national programme officers, and a junior professional officer. The office has eight support staff.

Program of Assistance: UNFPA funds a total of 14 projects in Tanzania. The largest project is a two-year, $3 million activity to develop a new Reproductive Health and Family Planning strategy, strengthen training in family planning, and expand family planning services. Other service-related projects seek to educate male workers about family planning; establish a family planning training center at the major national teaching hospital; and improve family planning and maternal health services in Zanzibar. UNFPA also funds a number of projects which aim to strengthen family life education in schools, teacher's colleges, and community development training institutions. Other projects seek to strengthen the capacity for population and development planning within both the national Planning Commission and the government of Zanzibar and to provide training in demographic and gender analysis at the University of Dar es Salaam. Two projects support the use of radio in family health education.

UNFPA Partners: UNFPA works primarily with the public sector but with a diversity of institutions. These include three different ministries — Health; Education and Culture; and Community Development, Women's Affairs and Children. Other implementing agencies include the Prime Minister's Office, the Planning Commission, the government of Zanzibar, the University of Dar es Salaam, the national trade union, and Radio Tanzania.

technical knowledge and capacity-building. In the short-term, UNFPA could develop contracts with international NGOs and firms, giving priority to those groups willing to work in collaboration with developing country NGOs and consulting firms. Progressively, developing country groups will develop capacity to handle direct contracts with UNFPA field offices. UNFPA should also seek to expand current south-to-south government partnerships to include private sector expertise.

By tapping into a broader pool of talent and increasing competition, the expanded use of international NGOs would also increase pressure on WHO and other UN agencies participating in the present technical support system to be more responsive to the needs of UNFPA and individual countries. It will take a change in UNFPA's culture to accelerate this process — a change needing encouragement from UNFPA's Executive Board and headquarters leadership.

5. Addressing the Growing Demand for Contraceptive Supplies

The ICPD Programme of Action projects a growing need for contraceptive supplies in developing countries. The number of couples in developing countries using family planning more than doubled from 1970 to 1980, and increased again substantially to 450 million in 1994. Estimates prepared for the ICPD suggest that, if current trends continue and demand for family planning is fully satisfied, family planning services will need to serve more than 650 million couples in developing countries, Eastern Europe and the former Soviet Republics by the year 2000.

Given this growing demand, many poor countries have relied to varying degrees on donor assistance to maintain an adequate choice of contraceptive methods and a reliable pipeline of good quality supplies. Foreign exchange and fiscal constraints make it difficult for many governments to purchase contraceptives with their own funds. Local manufacture is often not cost-effective, either because the market is too small or because the manufacturing process is too sophisticated for the local setting. In many poor countries, donated supplies also make it easier for cash strapped governments to provide subsidized services to consumers who could not pay the full commercial price.

The need for large numbers of condoms for AIDS prevention is also boosting developing country contraceptive requirements. In recent years, the WHO Global Programme on AIDS was a major supplier of condoms to developing countries, but its successor, the new UNAIDS program, appears unlikely to take on this role.

Moreover, as programs mature, contraceptive commodity needs are changing. Developing countries with large domestic markets are exploring the possibility of manufacturing contraceptives locally. This invariably requires the cooperation of established contraceptive manufacturers in technology transfer; the major multinational firms, consequently, have an important role to play. UNFPA has also helped in the transfer of contraceptive production technology to a number of countries and in the construction of contraceptive factories in India, Indonesia, China and Vietnam. In addition, UNFPA has supplied raw materials to local factories in these and other countries.

In the past, the United States was by far the largest source of donated contraceptive supplies. In the early 1990s, USAID provided over $60 million in contraceptives annually, or roughly three-fourths of total contraceptive commodity assistance. For

UNFPA has helped in the transfer of contraceptive production technology to a number of countries and in the construction of contraceptive factories.

years, USAID was the only donor assisting countries in systematically planning their contraceptive needs and strengthening distribution systems. USAID's withdrawal from some countries has left gaps not only in contraceptive supply but in the technical aspects of procurement planning and logistics management, where many countries still have limited capacity.

Recently, the volume of contraceptives procured by UNFPA has increased dramatically. In 1988, UNFPA provided $9.8 million in contraceptive commodity assistance. In 1994, the value of contraceptives procured by UNFPA reached $82 million, more than that provided by USAID or any other international donor. UNFPA also now has logistics advisors on each of the country support teams and is increasingly assisting countries in strengthening their contraceptive distribution networks.

This increase in procurement partly reflects UNFPA's role in helping national governments and other donors benefit from the economies of bulk contraceptive procurement by serving as their procurement agent. In 1994, roughly 40 percent of UNFPA's procurement was financed by external sources. The World Bank, for example, currently finances contraceptives in population and health projects in over 20 countries. It has used UNFPA's procurement services in cases where governments are unfamiliar with contraceptive procurement, and where the volume is too small for countries to obtain competitive prices on the international market. Other bilateral donors and a few developing country governments have also used UNFPA's procurement services. Donor agencies and governments pay a five percent handling charge, which to date has been credited to UNFPA's general resources rather than applied to procurement activities.

There has been general agreement within the international community that UNFPA is the appropriate agency to take the lead in addressing global contraceptive commodity needs. As part of an effort to respond to these needs, UNFPA established a working group on contraceptive commodity assistance which includes USAID, the British and German governments, the World Bank and IPPF. The Fund has also undertaken studies of current and long-term contraceptive requirements and logistics management needs in key developing countries, as well as global projections of contraceptive needs.

Weaknesses in procurement: UNFPA has made major strides in recent years in assuming greater leadership in contraceptive commodity assistance. Nevertheless, UNFPA's current procurement systems are not adequate to meet the growing demand for its services. To date, UNFPA has responded to requests on a country-by-country basis, handling each order for contraceptives individually rather than forecasting needs in advance and negotiating contracts for consolidated orders. Delays in shipment and interruptions in supply have occurred both as a result of UNFPA's own requirement that it have funds in hand prior to initiating a procurement, and the increasing lead time required by manufacturers of certain contraceptives. As a result, in the words of one expert, UNFPA too often "buys the wrong things, buys too much or too little, delivers items at the wrong time, and has not benefited enough from economies of scale."

UNFPA's existing contraceptive procurement unit is widely regarded as competent, but it is too small for its rapidly growing workload. In the past five years, the volume of procurement has quadrupled, while the staff has grown from 10 to 13. The

UNFPA is the appropriate agency to take the lead in addressing global contraceptive commodity needs.

UNFPA's current procurement systems are not adequate to meet the growing demand for its services.

lack of adequate capacity has contributed to procurement bottlenecks and prevented the unit from actively promoting its services to other donors and developing countries.

Limited scope of new initiatives: In 1995, UNFPA presented its Executive Board with two alternate proposals to enhance its capacity for commodity assistance. The Executive Board chose a relatively low cost approach to strengthening the existing procurement system over a more ambitious proposal. In 1996, the Board approved a $5 million revolving fund to enable the Fund to place advance orders and maintain buffer stocks to anticipate demand, as well as to respond rapidly to emergency requests. It also authorized UNFPA to hire limited additional procurement staff and to introduce an up-to-date computerized information system to improve monitoring and management of procurement actions.

These developments are encouraging. However, the need for a global contraceptive facility has been growing in recent years. Until recently, UNFPA's leadership appeared reluctant to expand its assistance in this area, perhaps perceiving potentially unlimited demand. A few donor countries on the Executive Board have also resisted expansion of the Fund's role in this area. The plan approved by the Board is a pilot effort of modest scope relative to existing needs. Thus, the Fund, while moving forward, has yet to address the growing need for contraceptives in a bold and vigorous way.

Recommendation #5: UNFPA needs to further expand its contraceptive commodity assistance and strengthen its capacity as a global contraceptive procurement agency. UNFPA's leadership and Executive Board need to take a long-term view and recognize the importance of adequate and affordable contraceptive supplies to the success of family planning programs.

If the current initiative proceeds smoothly, the Executive Board should consider increasing the value of the revolving fund substantially. A larger fund would allow reorganization of the budget process to shift to a system of estimating needs in advance and making consolidated procurements.

To support this shift, UNFPA needs additional procurement expertise in projecting contraceptive supply needs and advance planning of procurements. UNFPA has already taken on a greater role in contraceptive supply — now it needs to build the corresponding capacity to project, plan and manage an increased volume of procurements. Approval of new staff positions is delicate at a time of system-wide cutbacks. However, the importance of the task justifies an increase in core or project-funded personnel. The procurement unit could support the costs of additional personnel, if the fees on procurements for outside agencies were to revert to the unit.

UNFPA also needs to develop mechanisms to help developing countries build their own capacity in procurement planning and logistics management. Use of external expertise could help UNFPA respond more quickly and flexibly to requests for help and minimize the need to hire large numbers of new staff. The U.S. Centers for Disease Control and John Snow, Inc., for example, have a proven track record in providing hands-on assistance in contraceptive procurement planning and logistics management for USAID. UNFPA needs to develop similar mechanisms to supplement headquarters staff and the logistics advisors on the country support teams with broader institutional expertise. Again, these technical services could be financed through the fees on outside agency procurement.

UNFPA needs to more actively market its procurement services. While the Fund has a need to balance the allocation of its own internal funds between commodities and programs, there is essentially no limit — other than staff capacity — on the volume of procurement services it can provide to other donor agencies and developing countries. Developing countries on the Executive Board have been enthusiastic about the new initiative, suggesting a significant demand for this service. UNFPA must, however, take care to avoid discouraging the expansion of commercial manufacturers into developing country markets — which is important over the long-term to increase cost recovery through the private sector.

6. Staffing for Success: Strengthening Operational Capacity

As UNFPA strives to meet the challenges elaborated above, it must assess the adequacy of its own capacity to support implementation of the ICPD agenda. As a UN fund, UNFPA has more flexibility than the central UN bureaucracy in hiring personnel. Unlike the Secretariat, UNFPA is not bound by rigid national quotas, although as a UN entity it still pays attention to the mix of its staff and to representation of major donor countries in its senior management level. However, the Executive Board must approve changes in staffing patterns and any new positions.

Recognizing the recent growth in UNFPA's program budget, in an unprecedented step in late 1995 UNFPA's Executive Board approved 82 new positions for the 1996 to 1997 funding cycle. As a result of this action, UNFPA has a total of 919 approved positions. Of these, 240 (26%) are assigned to the Fund's headquarters in New York; the remaining 679 staff (74%) are assigned to UNFPA offices overseas. Roughly half of all UNFPA's overseas staff are in Africa.

Sixty-six of UNFPA's 98 field offices are headed by country representatives; in the other countries, UNDP resident representatives oversee national staff who manage UNFPA programs and projects. A typical country office includes some combination of a country representative, international program officers, and national program and support staff.

Thinness of professional field staff: *UNFPA's professional staff, like its funding, have been spread very thinly across field offices, limiting the Fund's capacity for effective program design, implementation and monitoring.* With the recent increase in posts, UNFPA has a total of 224 professional positions overseas, an average of only slightly over two staff for every field office. The total size of a field office averages about seven staff, including all support personnel. Staffing problems have been most acute in Africa, where local management capacity is also weak.

UNFPA has a total of 224 professional positions overseas, an average of only slightly over two staff for every field office.

UNFPA Staff by Category and Location, 1996			
	New York	**Field Offices**	**Total**
Professional	105	224	**329**
General Service	135	455	**590**
Total	**240**	**679***	**919**
*Includes 4 staff in Geneva.			**Source:** UNFPA

> *UNICEF has three times the budget and eight times the staff of UNFPA.*

The current staffing pattern places a great responsibility on the country representatives. As the 1993 evaluation noted, "the Country Director (Representative) is often the only international resource in the field office." UNFPA lacks a middle tier of international professional staff who can transfer program experiences and innovations from one country to another; there are only 15 international program officer posts worldwide. Since 1991, field offices have benefited from periodic visits by international experts on the country support teams. However, these experts are often unavailable unless scheduled well in advance and have not alleviated the basic shortage of staff.

Yet the expansion of international staff is hard to justify given the small size of many UNFPA country programs. International salaries represent a high proportion of field office overhead, largely because UNFPA has high fixed costs relative to small country budgets. As a cost saving measure, UNFPA has relied on national program staff, who have a generally favorable reputation, although some government counterparts have been reluctant to recognize their authority. Most of the recently-approved posts are designated for national hires; over two-thirds are for general service or support staff, and less than a third for professional personnel.

The thinness of professional staff has meant that many country representatives are overburdened with mundane paper work. It has also precluded field offices from having resident staff with specialized expertise to manage more sophisticated projects or engage in technical discussions with other donors and with governments. UNFPA does not have significant substantive expertise at the country level in contrast, for example, to UNICEF with its reputation as a leader in child health.

While UNICEF enjoys a reputation as the most effective UN implementing agency, it has three times the budget and eight times the staff of UNFPA. UNFPA, with a worldwide staff of some 900 compared to UNICEF's staff of 7,000, lacks the capacity to replicate UNICEF's operational style — an outcome which in any event may not be desirable given the criticism that UNICEF's staff and insistence on "doing it themselves" impede local capacity-building. Nonetheless, as a former UNFPA official notes: "The example of UNICEF shows that without adequate, qualified staff, you can't decentralize, let governments implement programs, demand full accountability, and make top quality inputs."

Inadequate headquarters support for field programs: At UNFPA headquarters in New York, the executive director is assisted by two deputies: one responsible for oversight of programs, the other for policy and administration. Substantive program functions are the responsibility of the Technical and Evaluation Division, which represents UNFPA's critical mass of technical expertise; and four geographic divisions, which provide routine backstopping of country programs. In addition, vital administrative functions are handled by the Division for Finance, Personnel and Administration; the Division of Information and External Relations; and the Programme Coordination, Management and Field Support Office.

There are two major issues relating to UNFPA's headquarters staff. *The first is that they are engaged in many tasks that consume valuable time and resources, but do not directly support the Fund's field programs. The second is that headquarters personnel are spread over many functions, limiting the depth of the Fund's technical capacity.*

With roughly one-fourth of the Fund's overall staff, UNFPA headquarters contrasts with the meager staffing in the country offices. However, as the focal point for population policy and programs within the UN system, UNFPA is expected by the international community to fulfill a heavy workload and broad range of functions relating to global advocacy and the larger UN system.

The ICPD process, while highly successful, absorbed the time of large numbers of headquarters staff for a period of almost three years. Subsequent UN conferences have placed further demands on UNFPA staff. The follow-up to the ICPD and other conferences has also been time consuming. Meetings of such UN intergovernmental bodies as the Economic and Social Council and the Commission on Population and Development further require the participation of UNFPA staff.

In addition, meetings of the joint UNDP-UNFPA Executive Board, and the reporting and information needs of the Board, represent a major drain on staff time. The 1993 donor evaluation had recommended that the Board meet less frequently than its previous, week-long, annual meetings. However, the UNDP-UNFPA Board now meets *four* times a year, reflecting the insistence by the Nordic countries on more frequent meetings for the Executive Boards of all UN funds engaged in operational development activities.

The focus at UNFPA headquarters on global advocacy and internal UN coordination and reporting diverts attention and resources from effective support to field programs. During the 1993 evaluation, country offices visited by the team reported receiving inadequate managerial and technical support from New York. While the authority delegated to country representatives has increased significantly, the full benefits of decentralization appear difficult to realize in the absence of both adequate field staff and support from headquarters. The limited exchange of staff between headquarters and country offices has further contributed to the weak field orientation, although recent appointments of field staff to senior positions in New York suggest this may change.

Moreover, UNFPA has a very thin layer of in-house specialized expertise in key areas such as the delivery of reproductive health services, evaluation, human resources planning, and program financing within a larger context of health financing and reform. For example, the Fund's Reproductive Health branch has just four professional staff to provide technical oversight for the Fund's 150 country programs in reproductive health and family planning. Technical specialists at headquarters also often spend substantial time preparing documents for various intergovernmental bodies, again at the cost of support to the field.

The Fund's ability to develop a stronger technical cadre in key program areas is constrained by the limited number of staff positions — only 105 of 240 headquarters posts are designated for professional personnel. These professional staff are spread across a broad range of functions. Some experts have recommended that UNFPA reallocate staff positions from New York to the field. However, it appears difficult for UNFPA to do so and still adequately staff vital headquarters functions such as global advocacy and fundraising, technical leadership, and field office backstopping, in addition to necessary financial and administrative functions.

Thus, while the approval of a significant number of new positions in late 1995 represents an important step towards strengthening UNFPA staffing, professional staff are still

> *UNFPA is expected to fulfill a heavy workload relating to global advocacy and the larger UN system.*

> *The dispersion of staff resources in both the country offices and at headquarters remains a chronic problem, undermining UNFPA's effectiveness at all levels.*

thinly stretched, especially in the field. The dispersion of staff resources in both the country offices and at headquarters remains a chronic problem, undermining UNFPA's effectiveness at all levels.

Recommendation #6: If UNFPA is to become a more significant operational force at the country level, it needs to strengthen field office staffing and reorient headquarters staff to increase support to country programs.

UNFPA's Executive Board and leadership need to review the current allocation of overseas staff positions, redeploying human resources to countries with the greatest need and supplementing existing staff where necessary with additional hires. In the final analysis, staffing patterns must be cost-effective relative to the allocation of program resources. It remains hard to justify increases in international staff in the field offices without a greater concentration of UNFPA funds in key program countries. A redeployment of staff would logically follow such a concentration of resources.

The concentration of funds in fewer countries would also likely increase the ratio of program to administrative costs, improving the cost-effectiveness of UNFPA's field operations. While such a redeployment would minimize the need for additional hires, the Board should remain open to gradually adding professional positions, including more mid-level national and international staff, to enhance field office technical and managerial capabilities.

UNFPA's leadership needs to find ways to reorganize staff responsibilities at headquarters to increase support to the field. The 1993 evaluation sent a strong message on the need to restructure personnel and financial resources so that the "greatest part of the UNFPA program is dedicated to the improvement of country-level population and family planning programs as it is at that level that population problems are addressed..."

To accomplish this, UNFPA's leadership needs to find ways to reduce the amount of time headquarters staff spend servicing the internal requirements of the UN system. While it is not desirable for UNFPA to disengage from internal UN coordination activities, UNFPA needs to reorder priorities at headquarters to refocus on technical and field support functions for country programs. A decision by the Executive Board to revert to twice or even once yearly meetings — and to require fewer reports of UNFPA — would also contribute to such a shift.

UNFPA must do more to build expertise in key areas relating to the implementation of reproductive health programs. Given the greater claim of field offices on new staff positions, UNFPA should review the current personnel structure and consider the feasibility of converting some general service posts to professional positions. The Fund should also consider streamlining various headquarters functions to permit greater depth of technical staff in key areas. For example, it may be possible to strengthen the Fund's expertise in technical areas by consolidating the number of units within the Technical and Evaluation Division and reallocating staff positions to reproductive health and other key areas.

UNFPA should also place more emphasis on developing existing human resources. The Fund has been expanding in-service training and should further strengthen these efforts. It should give special emphasis to helping country representatives realize the full potential of their positions. As part of developing an improved career system, there should be regular rotation of professional staff between headquarters and the field and expanded opportunities for the promotion of good national program officers to international positions. The Fund should also competitively recruit a few outstanding junior professionals each year. Finally, the system should promote good performers and weed out the weak — difficult but not impossible within the UN system.

There should be regular rotation of professional staff between headquarters and the field.

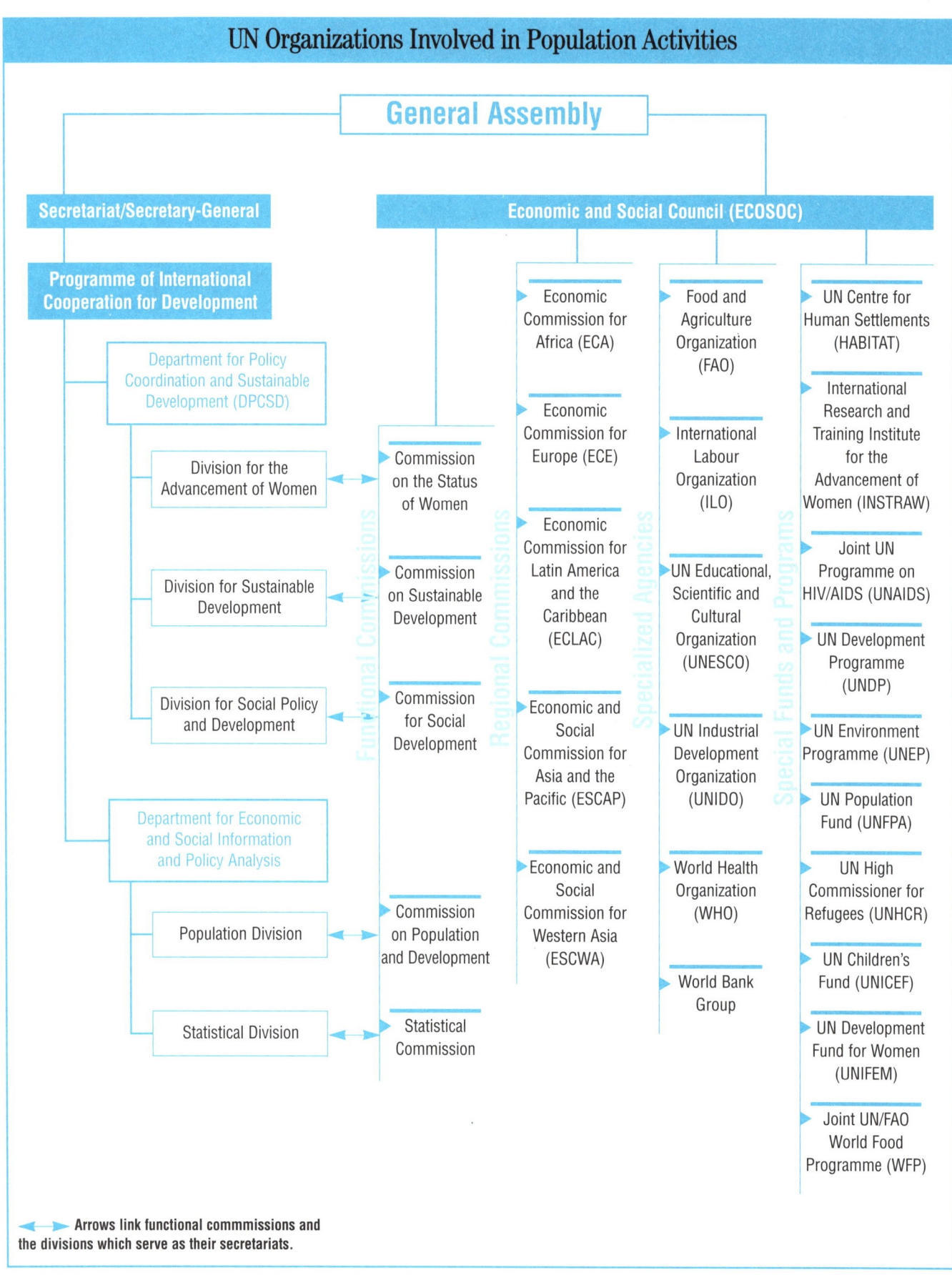

III. Building Synergy within the UN System

The Role of UNFPA in Interagency Coordination

The ICPD *Programme of Action* recognizes that population stabilization requires progress on a broad social and economic development agenda. UN organizations work in many different areas; given limited resources, it is important that their programs support population objectives to the extent consistent with their own mandates. Effective ICPD implementation requires complementarity and synergy among the population related programs of various UN organizations.

Despite concern about the effectiveness of the specialized agencies in implementing UNFPA-funded projects, UNFPA deserves credit for successfully engaging other UN agencies in population activities. Indeed, UNFPA has had substantial influence on the rest of the UN system, underscoring the importance of having a UN organization with an exclusive mandate to work on population.

Looking to the future, UNFPA has a continuing role to play in leading the UN system in support of the ICPD Programme of Action. This role extends beyond UNFPA's limited funding of the population activities of other UN entities. At the policy level, UNFPA's goal should be to encourage the entire system to engage in sustained advocacy aimed at stimulating more comprehensive and effective national action to address population problems. At the program level, coordination is important to ensure that each organization plays to its comparative advantage, given the functional specialization of the UN system.

Yet UNFPA's ability to forge effective partnerships is limited by the capacity and commitment of other UN organizations. Population and reproductive health is marginal to the mainstream work of many UN agencies, who have historically seen UNFPA primarily as a supplementary source of funds for their own bureaucracies. Despite some changes since the ICPD, most lack a deep commitment to population issues and remain reluctant to spend funds from their increasingly constrained core budgets on population activities.

Progress and Constraints Relating to Interagency Collaboration

Beginning before the ICPD, the UN system has made a serious attempt to improve coordination of its development activities, with a focus on the field level. Nevertheless, efforts to improve coordination of the UN's development programs — including its population activities — face an uphill battle.

Lack of Effective Global Coordination: *In reality, there is no central oversight or coordination of the UN's development efforts.* An estimated 100 legally separate UN entities are involved in every sphere of human activity. Yet, only the Secretary-General has authority over the funds, commissions, and heads of economic and social departments. Neither the Secretary-General nor any other body has real authority over all the specialized agencies, which operate independently of UN headquarters in New York and report to their own governing assemblies. Although a multitude of interagency committees are charged with improving coordination, "…because of organizational turf battles or a lack of resources, the existing machinery simply has not worked and very little effective coordination actually occurs within the UN system," says a recent analysis.

In a helpful development, the Secretary-General has tasked the administrator of UNDP, the lead agency for the UN's development

Effective ICPD implementation requires complementarity and synergy among the population related programs of various UN organizations.

activities, with improving coordination among the UN organizations engaged in development activities. Yet although there has been talk of upgrading this position to a Deputy Secretary-General for Development, at present this position has no real line or management authority over the other funds and programs.

Mixed Progress on Country-Level Coordination: *The proliferation of separate funds and agencies has contributed to excessive compartmentalization on the one hand, and to overlapping mandates and duplication of effort on the other. At the country level, all agencies still develop programs separately in a piecemeal approach.* Advocates of reform recommend combining the UN's development activities into a single country program; while this is unlikely to happen, most experts agree on the need for closer collaboration on the development of complementary programs.

Since 1993, at the urging of the General Assembly, the UN has attempted to strengthen the role of the UN resident coordinator (usually the UNDP representative). As the local head of the UN system, the resident coordinator has overall responsibility for coordinating the activities of UN agencies present in a given country. Recent initiatives include introduction of a common "country strategy note" for the whole UN system, intended as a framework for articulating national development priorities and permitting the resident coordinator to orchestrate inputs from the different UN funds and agencies. UNFPA, UNICEF and UNDP have also harmonized funding cycles for most of their programs.

The decision to give UNFPA country directors the title of country representative, putting UNFPA on a par with other UN organizations, has further improved prospects for effective coordination and ICPD implementation. Previously, UNFPA field representatives lacked equal status with the field representatives of other UN entities and the authority to receive government requests for assistance, placing them at a disadvantage in policy and program discussions at the country level.

Nevertheless, interagency collaboration at the country level remains uneven. The introduction of country notes and the move to harmonize funding cycles have been less than fully successful. Turf concerns on the part of the various agencies continue to constrain the authority of the resident coordinators. Interaction between organizations at the country level also remains too much a function of individual personalities.

ICPD Follow-up Activities: *The ICPD has fostered dialogue and improved cohesion on population issues within the UN system.* The headquarters staff of various UN agencies have spent significant time and effort on ICPD follow-up activities, including the Inter-Agency Task Force on ICPD Implementation, and the six Task Force working groups. In early 1996, the Task Force was folded into a new Task Force on Basic Social Services for All, combining follow-up functions for all the recent international conferences.

The ICPD task force developed a "Common Advocacy Statement on Population and Development" for the entire UN system. In late 1995, the Administrative Committee on Coordination, the highest level UN coordinating body, approved the statement, giving it an official imprimatur.

The ICPD task force also prepared guidelines on themes relating to ICPD implementation and distributed these to UN resident coordinators at the country level. The guidelines are intended to educate resident coordi-

> *At the country level, all UN agencies still develop programs separately in a piecemeal approach.*

nators on how to operationalize the ICPD *Programme of Action* and promote integrated planning of UN inputs. They address the themes of reproductive health, women's empowerment, and basic education, with special emphasis on equalizing access for girls. The guidelines however, are very general and lack a strong action orientation. It is too early to assess whether these headquarters initiatives will lead to more coordinated programming at the country level.

Implementing ICPD: UNFPA and the Role of Other UN Agencies

The problems of inter-agency coordination described above inevitably constrain UNFPA's efforts to advance the ICPD *Programme of Action*. Solutions to many of these problems require far-ranging reforms of the UN system. Nevertheless, there are steps that UNFPA and the other UN agencies could take to work together more effectively. The following section explores the opportunities for greater complementarity between the activities of UNFPA and other UN organizations in three areas critical to ICPD implementation: reproductive health and family planning; the social and economic advancement of women; and population policy development.

1. Strengthening Reproductive Health and Family Planning: Collaborating with WHO and UNICEF

Following the ICPD, a central challenge for UNFPA and the UN system is to support national efforts to implement reproductive health and family planning programs. Although UNFPA is the key operational agency in this area, WHO and UNICEF have important contributions to make. However, neither organization has fully realized its potential contribution.

WHO and Technical Leadership: WHO has a broad mandate relating to human health and to international cooperation on public health problems. In recent years, it has focused on providing strategic guidance to governments to achieve the mission of "health for all by the year 2000," with a strong emphasis on primary care. WHO views reproductive health and family planning as one element of primary care.

WHO's most significant contribution has been as a technical leader. A considerable part of its role is normative and informational — formulating international health standards, disseminating information, and providing advice to governments on technologies and program approaches. It also plays an important role in developing health statistics and in scientific exchange.

WHO has been less involved in carrying out field programs. In the 1970s, WHO was the leader in global campaigns to eradicate specific diseases such as smallpox. More recently, however, severe budget constraints have limited staff and funds for country operations. A further problem undermining WHO's effectiveness at the field level is the lack of effective coordination between WHO headquarters in Geneva and its essentially independent regional offices. WHO headquarters has limited influence over the regional offices, which oversee country programs.

The UN system has designated WHO as the lead agency in reproductive health. WHO's Special Programme for Research, Development and Research Training in Human Reproduction (HRP), funded from voluntary contributions, has been an international leader in research relating to contraceptive development, introduction and safety issues. WHO's former Family Health

The weak coordination between WHO headquarters and regional offices has constrained field level effectiveness.

> *In recent years, UNICEF has recognized reproductive health and family planning as part of a comprehensive approach to child survival and safe motherhood.*

Division also included units working on family planning and adolescent and maternal health.

As part of ICPD follow-up, WHO has taken some steps to increase the visibility of reproductive health within the organization. In 1995, it announced a new reproductive health strategy emphasizing advocacy, research, technical leadership and support to country programs. In a major reorganization in 1996, WHO established a new Family and Reproductive Health program, which seeks to strengthen technical support in reproductive health and to link the human reproduction research program more closely with technical support functions.

Some observers have questioned the depth of WHO's commitment to reproductive health, which must compete for attention within the organization with other areas of health. WHO allocates very limited funds from its regular budget to reproductive health activities; extra-budgetary resources — including funds from UNFPA — continue to support most WHO staff and activities in this area. Still, the recent restructuring is an important sign of commitment to reproductive health.

UNICEF's Advocacy and Field Programs: In contrast to WHO, UNICEF — the UN agency responsible for child health and welfare — has developed into a strong, action-oriented development agency with a large budget and field presence. UNICEF's staff and infrastructure at the country level are a powerful delivery system for a broad range of social services.

UNICEF allocates about one-fourth of its funds to health programs, and its greatest successes have been in child health. The scope of its activities extends more broadly to many aspects of the ICPD plan of action, including adolescent health, infant and child health, safe motherhood, girls' education, and women's development programs.

UNICEF has potential to make a significant contribution in reproductive health and family planning. It has a large cadre of health specialists; its programs reach large numbers of women; as a major supplier of drugs and vaccines it has considerable expertise in commodity assistance; and it has been an influential advocate for other critical child health interventions with political leaders.

In the past, however, UNICEF's maternal and child health programs gave virtually no emphasis to reproductive health and family planning. UNICEF priorities have been set by a Board which has been reluctant to play a substantial role in this area. Some governments on UNICEF's Board support family planning and women's health in principle but believe the Fund should focus on child health while other agencies work in these areas. The Vatican, conservative members of the U.S. Congress, and U.S. anti-abortion groups have also worked for years to prevent UNICEF's involvement in family planning and have criticized UNICEF for its involvement in efforts to prevent unsafe abortion.

More recently, especially following the ICPD and the advent of new leadership, UNICEF's posture has been changing. Especially at the policy level, UNICEF has played a more constructive role vis-a-vis population and family planning. In strategic documents in recent years, UNICEF has recognized reproductive health and family planning as part of a comprehensive approach to child survival and safe motherhood. This rhetorical support is important, given UNICEF's prestige in most developing countries.

In the past, with ambivalent guidance from headquarters, UNICEF country offices were unwilling to be too closely associated with family planning, especially in Latin America where UNICEF has been sensitive to the concerns of the Catholic church. In the face of continuing political pressure, UNICEF remains generally reluctant to include family planning in its field programs.

UNICEF, however, is a highly decentralized agency, and some country offices have taken a more proactive role in reproductive health and family planning. UNICEF has recently given high priority to reducing maternal mortality and has expanded its involvement in adolescent health. Some 30 country programs now support special reproductive health initiatives, which in a few cases include family planning. However, the main thrust of UNICEF's maternal health programs has emphasized improved obstetrical care; adolescent initiatives have stressed AIDS prevention.

WHO and UNICEF— Collaboration with UNFPA: To varying degrees, WHO and UNICEF cooperate with UNFPA in policy development, technical exchange, and joint programming in reproductive health.

Policy Development: In the past, the three organizations often had difficulty coordinating policy at the country level. However, in 1991, the heads of WHO, UNICEF, UNFPA and UNDP signed a joint letter on maternal-child health and family planning, urging field staff to plan and coordinate their activities more closely. More recently, the Task Force for ICPD follow-up — in particular the working group on reproductive health — has provided a mechanism for increased policy coordination. UNFPA has also suggested that the three organizations hold regular high level consultations to agree on a joint health policy framework, a process which could help identify opportunities for increased collaboration on reproductive and child health programs.

Technical Exchange: Given its limited technical capacity, UNFPA has looked to WHO for technical inputs in support of its country-level programs. The Fund has provided funding to both the human reproduction research program and the former Family Health Division.

WHO's response reflects a mixed picture. The research program has established a strong reputation for scientific excellence and has provided UNFPA with authoritative advice on contraceptive technology issues. UNFPA has also relied on the family planning standards and guidelines developed by WHO's former Family Health division — for example, standards for clinical care and eligibility criteria for contraceptive use. The adolescent and maternal health programs within the division have further provided leadership in their respective areas.

Overall, however, WHO has demonstrated limited capacity to provide technical support to UNFPA at the country level. As a recent study aptly states, in each country WHO generally has "a single professional staff member who, armed with little power to make decisions and few resources, is responsible for overseeing a broad range of WHO's initiatives." WHO representatives look to the semi-autonomous WHO regional offices for guidance and direction.

WHO has fielded technical experts in reproductive health on UNFPA's country support teams and has trained team members on reproductive health issues. Especially in Africa, however, it has failed to fill key positions in a timely manner. Although the research program has a worldwide network of collaborating institutions, its current structure does not encourage the application of its scientific expertise to promote better

UNICEF has been generally reluctant to include family planning in its field programs.

WHO, UNICEF and UNFPA collaborate more closely at headquarters than at the field level.

policies relating to contraceptive technologies at the national level.

It is too early to gauge the impact of the recent reorganization of reproductive health functions on WHO's capacity for technical support. Some observers remain skeptical that this restructuring can overcome the bifurcation of leadership and program responsibility between WHO headquarters and its regional offices. These deeper organizational problems remain a major constraint to WHO's ability to serve as a strong partner to UNFPA at the field level.

Program Coordination: At headquarters, the three organizations collaborate on various global initiatives. For example, they are all co-sponsors — along with UNESCO, UNDP and the World Bank — of the recently established Joint UN Programme on HIV/AIDS (UNAIDS), which replaced the Global Programme on AIDS in early 1996 and represents a new model of interagency collaboration.

At the country level, overall, there is relatively little direct program collaboration, reflecting both WHO's operational weakness and UNICEF's preference for programmatic autonomy. In general, UNICEF has had a special working relationship with WHO, but UNICEF and UNFPA have also had joint projects in a few countries. Patterns of collaboration have also varied by region. In Latin America, both UNICEF and UNFPA work closely with the Pan American Health Organization, the WHO regional affiliate. In Africa, WHO's weak capacity has limited opportunities for collaboration. In addition, both WHO and UNICEF representatives in some countries have been weak advocates for family planning and have not been interested in closer collaboration with UNFPA.

The 1993 donor evaluation of UNFPA perceived the lack of active collaboration between UNICEF and UNFPA in programming and advocacy for family planning as detrimental to the effectiveness of the world-wide family planning effort. Although the situation is changing, the strength of UNICEF's field operations continues to represent significant untapped potential for closer collaboration between the two organizations.

Recommendation #7: There is substantial potential for UNICEF, WHO and UNFPA to work together in the reproductive health field in a more complementary way. Agency heads should hold a summit to agree on how the three organizations can work on new challenges together and develop a more mutually supportive division of labor; they should meet annually to monitor progress. They also need to send strong messages to country offices to encourage them to collaborate more closely and to create incentives for increased collaboration.

Both UNICEF and WHO can do much more to support UNFPA's work through advocacy. WHO's reproductive health strategy appropriately identifies advocacy as an area for action; a critical challenge is to convince health ministers and the medical establishment — constituencies over which WHO has some influence — to increase the priority assigned to reproductive health, both within the overall health sector and within primary health services.

UNICEF, too, has significant leverage with health officials and can make a major contribution by promoting the importance of reproductive health, including family planning, in ongoing advocacy, even if its involvement in programs remains limited. UNICEF could do much more to publicize the well-established impact of family planning in lowering infant and maternal mortality. Both UNICEF and WHO could also do more, working in tandem with UNFPA, to educate policymakers on the vital need for sexuality education and reproductive health services for young people, a controversial issue in many countries.

WHO should pursue its current efforts to strengthen technical guidance to UNFPA in its operational role and to provide greater leadership at the country level in translating the concept of reproductive health into effective programs. To fulfill this role, WHO must assign high priority to issues relating to the integration of reproductive health within primary health systems. The reproductive health technical support unit within WHO must take the lead in assembling data on the cost and effectiveness of alternative reproductive health interventions and delivery systems. While other national and private agencies are also working on these issues, governments continue to look to WHO as an authoritative and neutral source of expert advice.

The research program on human reproduction, meanwhile, should continue its outstanding work, expanding the scope of its activities to include the development of broader reproductive health technologies. Both the research program and the technical support unit also need to develop the capacity to provide analysis and advice to individual countries and to help UNFPA address technical problems and influence policies at the national level. If WHO is unable, owing to its own internal structural constraints, to provide UNFPA and developing countries with the technical guidance needed for effective program implementation, UNFPA will need to obtain these services from outside the UN system, as discussed in Chapter II above.

UNICEF and UNFPA need to explore possibilities for joint programming in reproductive and child health on a country by country basis. Given UNICEF's involvement in reproductive health and women's programs, it has great potential to complement the work of UNFPA. Models for such collaboration already exist in a few countries where UNFPA has supported family planning services alongside UNICEF-funded village-based maternal-child health programs. UNICEF could also make an important contribution by including contraceptives in its essential drug and commodity programs and assisting with the management of supplies, in countries where it has a comparative advantage in this area over UNFPA.

The recent collaboration on reproductive health between UNFPA and the UN High Commissioner for Refugees represents a good model for collaboration between UNICEF and UNFPA. The heads of the two organizations have signed an agreement committing their organizations to joint action to respond to reproductive health needs in emergency situations. The organizations subsequently sponsored a joint workshop to identify appropriate program approaches and developed materials to disseminate program guidelines. Country representatives from both agencies are now exploring the potential for complementary field-level programs.

2. Enhancing Links Between Population, Women and Development: Complementing the Work of Other UN Agencies

The ICPD Programme of Action recognizes that improvements in the status of women contribute to the success of population programs. The *Programme* calls for expanded educational and economic opportunities for women, both to enhance the lives of individual women and as a strategy for creating an enabling social and economic climate for fertility decline. The Beijing conference *Platform for Action* further elaborates an agenda

UNICEF could do much more to publicize the well-established impact of family planning in lowering infant and maternal mortality.

The UN lacks effective institutions to ensure implementation of the women's development agenda.

for advancing the social, economic, legal and political status of women.

While the ICPD and Beijing Conference provide a common agenda for the work of UN agencies in women's development, the UN lacks effective institutions to ensure implementation of this agenda.

UN bodies formally entrusted with promoting policies to advance the status of women include the Commission on the Status of Women (CSW), the UN Development Fund for Women (UNIFEM), and the International Research and Training Institute for the Advancement of Women (INSTRAW).

- The Commission on the Status of Women, which meets annually, works at the legal, political and legislative level. Its major accomplishment has been the Convention on the Elimination of All Forms of Discrimination Against Women, adopted by the General Assembly in 1979.

- The Division for the Advancement of Women in the UN Secretariat is the central unit within the UN for all matters relating to women. It serves as the secretariat for the Commission on the Status of Women and also organized the Beijing conference on women.

- UNIFEM is the main UN operational agency focusing on women. Its mission is to provide technical and financial support to programs designed to improve women's status. However, with a 1995 budget of $11.6 million and a staff of 21, UNIFEM is ill-equipped to fulfill this mandate. It has directed its limited resources to small-scale income-generating projects for women.

- INSTRAW was set up in 1976 in the Dominican Republic as a training resource to support the role of women in development, but remains a marginal player.

- Other UN agencies also work on various aspects of women's development. Indeed, virtually every UN agency or department in the Secretariat has a unit working on women's issues.

As described by a former UNICEF official, "The main characteristics of these institutional arrangements are multiplicity of actors, diffused mandates, limited financial resources and inadequate interaction with national governments." The UN's weak institutions for women's development stand in sharp contrast to the strong organization it has created in UNICEF for its work on child health and welfare.

Moreover, while several women head up UN funds and programs, there are few women in high level positions in the central Secretariat. This has contributed to a vacuum in advocacy and leadership on women's issues at the top levels of the UN bureaucracy. Meanwhile, the UN system also lacks adequate funding for action programs to advance the status of women. UN member states and top officials alike have lacked the political will to push for more effective women's agencies.

The Beijing conference process generated several proposals to strengthen UN institutions in the area of women's development. Among these was a proposal for the creation of a new high level agency to elevate women's advancement on the UN's policy agenda and coordinate its work relating to women. Proponents of such a new agency envision an umbrella organization headed by an Under Secretary-General to oversee, support and coordinate existing UN institutions and programs relating to women's development.

Governments and NGOs at the Beijing conference, recognizing the UN's institutional weakness, asked the Secretary-General to appoint a high level official for women's issues within the Secretariat structure. This recommendation led to considerable internal bureaucratic conflict, as UN officials debated whether to retain the secretariat for the Beijing conference or create a new institutional structure.

The Secretary-General responded to proponents of an expanded UN role in women's development in late 1995 by naming a new coordinator for women's affairs for the United Nations system. The responsibilities of the position are broadly defined, ranging from gender issues relating to the UN's personnel system to support for women's development programs. However, the new coordinator for women's affairs still has no real authority over other UN organizations, nor does the position have access to the resources needed for large-scale programs to benefit women.

Given this vacuum in leadership within the rest of the UN system, UNFPA emerged during the ICPD process as one of the most vocal and active agencies working for women's development. Recognizing the mutually reinforcing nature of efforts to improve the lives of individual women and to accelerate fertility decline, UNFPA has broadened its involvement over the last several years in a range of women's concerns beyond access to maternal-child health and family planning services. It is increasingly an advocate for programs to improve educational access for girls, eliminate female genital mutilation, and expand access to credit for women.

Yet at a programmatic level, UNFPA's primary thrust remains the provision of reproductive health and contraceptive services. To provide financial support for the broader agenda of women's empowerment would risk diluting both UNFPA's focus and the limited resources available for reproductive health and family planning services. UNFPA has resolved these tensions by identifying advocacy as a major new area of program activity — a strategy which enables it to actively encourage a broad range of population related development interventions without providing direct program support.

Such UN agencies as UNESCO, ILO, and FAO also have a strong interest in and substantial expertise relating to women's development — UNESCO in girls' education, and ILO and FAO in women's economic participation. Yet UNFPA's support to these agencies has had a very different focus. ILO's population activities have emphasized employment-based family planning education and services, primarily aimed at men, while FAO has reached out to rural agricultural populations. UNESCO projects funded by UNFPA have emphasized population education. Yet with respect to implementation of the ICPD agenda, these agencies appear to have a greater potential contribution to make in the broader area of advancing women's development than through the activities for which they have traditionally received funds from UNFPA.

All three agencies have made internal organizational changes to elevate the priority accorded to population activities following the ICPD. Still, the willingness of these agencies to commit their own funds to these activities in the absence of UNFPA support remains unclear. Few staff are available for population work, since UNFPA funds for headquarters staff and overhead have declined under the new technical support arrangements. With donor countries reducing their voluntary contributions — and in some cases withholding core assessments — the agencies appear unlikely to allocate substantial resources from their own budgets for ICPD implementation.

UNFPA has broadened its involvement in a range of women's concerns beyond maternal-child health and family planning.

UNFPA must set clear boundaries between advocacy and large-scale funding for broader women's development programs.

Recommendation #8: UNFPA should continue to play a role in advocacy for women's empowerment, but other UN agencies must do more within their areas of specialization to support women's development efforts. Given the ICPD mandate, UNFPA country representatives need to more actively encourage the development of women's programs and a better division of labor with other UN agencies. The role of UNFPA, with its lack of expertise in this field, should be that of an advocate for expanded access to education for girls and other initiatives which benefit women and as a partner in planning for implementation of the broader ICPD agenda.

UNFPA must set clear boundaries between advocacy and large-scale funding for broader women's development programs. It should also reconsider its traditional partnerships in reproductive health and family planning with agencies such as ILO, FAO, and UNESCO, which have limited expertise in this area and a poor reputation for effectiveness. The UN resident coordinators, however, need to encourage these other agencies to commit their own resources to women's programs, in areas where their interests converge with ICPD goals. UNFPA should also consider instituting short training courses for UN resident coordinators and other UN agency representatives, to enhance understanding of both population issues and their potential role in ICPD implementation.

Finally, as part of long-term reform efforts, the UN system should develop more effective institutional arrangements to promote the interests of women. Such a new structure to advance the status of women should incorporate greater influence on policy, increased staff and funds for action programs to benefit women, and the authority to bring greater coherence to women's activities throughout the UN system.

3. Creating a Global Consensus on Population: Working with the UN Policy Machinery

Given the UN's influence in developing countries, the UN's intergovernmental policy machinery is an important potential vehicle for encouraging countries to support and implement the ICPD Programme of Action.

The major UN intergovernmental bodies involved in population policy development include the Economic and Social Council (ECOSOC), which has broad responsibility for coordinating the UN's development activities, and the Commission on Population and Development, which following ICPD was restructured and given a new mandate to monitor implementation of the ICPD *Programme of Action*.

Unfortunately, the UN's policy machinery is weak and ineffective in directing the activities of UN agencies in the areas of social and economic development. ECOSOC is responsible for oversight and coordination of all UN specialized agencies, funds and programs (including UNFPA), 14 regional and functional commissions (including the Commission on Population and Development), and 6 standing committees. With a membership of 54 countries, it is too unwieldy in size to effectively formulate social and economic policy. ECOSOC's annual meetings do not provide sufficient time to adequately address its broad mandate. ECOSOC has thus been unable to provide meaningful guidance or coordination to the UN's population activities; from an operational perspective, it has added little value to the UN's population activities and to most of its development work.

Nevertheless, ECOSOC serves some important governance functions in setting the parameters and mandates for other UN bodies involved in population and development. For example, it determined the size and terms of reference for the reconstituted Commission on Population and Development and set the overall agenda for the ICPD and other major UN conferences. The annual ECOSOC meeting also represents an opportunity for advocacy with member governments and other UN agencies. However, in the absence of larger reforms, which include an extension of its present working calendar, most observers believe it is not possible for ECOSOC to raise the profile of population issues at annual meetings.

The role of the Commission on Population and Development is changing. In the past, representation on the Commission, formerly called the Population Commission, consisted primarily of demographers who approved the biannual workplan for the Population Division's research program. The Commission also played a role in monitoring the World Population Plan of Action agreed on at the Bucharest population conference in 1974, as well as the recommendations drafted at the Mexico City conference in 1984. More recently, the General Assembly renamed the commission, expanded its membership, and broadened its role to include monitoring implementation of the ICPD *Programme of Action*.

The reconstituted Commission met for the first time in February, 1996, and is an evolving institution. Unlike the UNFPA Executive Board, which has governance functions over UNFPA operations, the Commission is charged with addressing the big picture relating to ICPD implementation and the links between the follow-up to ICPD and other recent UN conferences. The Commission is in a better position than the UNFPA Executive Board to frame policy recommendations for national governments and for consideration by higher level UN bodies such as the General Assembly. Moreover, the Commission provides broad policy direction and requires reporting by UN agencies, two important policy functions.

However, the Commission has yet to show whether it can be effective in monitoring operational programs. Although the composition of the Commission is changing to include more senior government officials, its visibility and clout appear likely to remain limited, in part, because representation of member states tends to be below the ministerial level. In addition, it has no direct authority over budgetary allocations or program decisions.

Other intergovernmental bodies also play — or could potentially play — a role in consensus-building and population policy development. The regional economic commissions have stimulated discussion of population issues at regional meetings. However, the involvement of the different commissions has varied greatly. The Economic and Social Commission for Asia and the Pacific (ESCAP) has been by far the most active in the population field; the other regional commissions have been less influential.

Among the UN functional commissions, the Commission on Sustainable Development and the Commission on the Status of Women could potentially play significant roles in encouraging decision-makers in other sectors to support population programs. The former monitors implementation of *Agenda 21*, the document agreed to at the Earth Summit in Rio de Janeiro in 1992, which includes a chapter on the links between population, environment and development. In 1997, UNFPA will

ECOSOC has been unable to provide meaningful guidance or coordination to the UN's population activities.

prepare a paper for the Commission on progress on population and development issues; the Commission will also hold a special session of the General Assembly to review progress on *Agenda 21*. Similarly, the Commission on the Status of Women has potential interest in women's reproductive health concerns.

Within the UN bureaucracy, the UN Population Division has played an important supporting role in policy development through data analysis, enhancing understanding and awareness of global and national population trends. The Division has played an important role in tracking demographic trends of all kinds — not only fertility and population growth, but also mortality, urbanization, and migration. Its population projections have been influential in convincing policymakers in many countries to initiate action programs to address rapid population growth. The Division has also undertaken regular monitoring and reporting of national population policies, including in the sensitive area of abortion. As an observer of global trends, the Division has developed a well-deserved reputation for professional excellence. Its independence and objectivity have been important strengths and contributed to its credibility.

The Division's location within the central UN bureaucracy has helped to integrate population issues into the UN's broader social and analytical functions. In its role as the secretariat for the Commission on Population and Development, the Division's workload has recently expanded significantly to include ICPD-related monitoring. However, its staff and funds have been eroding in the face of UN budget cuts. The Division also has little expertise relating to operational programs. While UNFPA has been an important source of funding for the Division's analytical work and assistance in data analysis to developing countries, there has been little day to day collaboration between the two agencies. Thus, links between the UN's analytical and operational work in the population field remain weak.

Notwithstanding the influence of the Population Division's analytical work, the decennial UN population conferences represent the most successful UN initiatives in the population policy arena. These conferences have played a major role in getting high level political leaders talking about population, in raising the visibility of population issues with the general public, and in legitimizing organized family planning efforts. They have helped to generate a consensus on appropriate program strategies and to educate leaders about these approaches. Especially in the 1990s, UN conferences have also been an effective and flexible vehicle through which the UN has been able to engage nongovernmental organizations in the policy process.

The recent ICPD, under UNFPA's dynamic leadership, had a particularly strong influence on policy. It revitalized faltering support for population programs by building a fresh consensus on values and approaches that broadened the constituency for these programs. The ICPD process stimulated several donor countries to significantly increase their population assistance. As a result of the ICPD, a number of developing countries are undertaking major new population and reproductive health initiatives.

Other international conferences, such as the Copenhagen Social Summit and the Beijing Fourth World Conference on Women, also have relevance to population policy development. Beyond the discussion in conference documents relating directly to population and family planning concerns, these conferences have rein-

> *The recent ICPD, under UNFPA's dynamic leadership, had a particularly strong influence on policy.*

forced the importance of such broader social issues as the role of women and girls' education. Recognizing the value of conferences in consensus building, UNFPA has proposed an international meeting in 1999 as a five year follow-up to the ICPD.

Recommendation #9: **The international community must work together to strengthen the more promising UN mechanisms for building consensus on population issues.**

UNFPA should invest only the minimum attention in ECOSOC needed to ensure that it performs its basic governance functions relating to the UN's population work. ECOSOC has very limited potential to contribute to consensus building on population issues or coordination of the UN's population activities.

UN member nations and the international community should closely monitor the effectiveness of the Commission on Population and Development. The Commission has potential but needs time to grow into its new and expanded role. The international population community also needs to assume some responsibility for making the Commission work better; more regular and active participation by NGOs, for example, would bring new energy and vitality to the Commission's annual meetings.

UNFPA and the population community, together with UN member nations, need to take the Commission on Sustainable Development and the Commission on the Status of Women more seriously as fora for consensus building on population related issues. These commissions represent an alternative channel with greater potential than ECOSOC for bringing population issues to the attention of a wider range of policymakers. Through their annual meetings and General Assembly reviews, these commissions could facilitate the long-term process of integrating population issues into overall development debates.

UNFPA and the Population Division need to increase collaboration, with a view to building stronger links between the policy and operational aspects of the UN's population work. UNFPA should increase the role of the Division in the preparation of analytical reports; it could contract with the Division for ongoing support in this area. This would strengthen UNFPA's analytical capacity, while at the same time enriching the Division's operational reporting to the Commission on Population and Development. Increased use of working groups including expertise from outside the UN system could also augment the capacities of both UNFPA and the Population Division in policy development.

Given the weaknesses of the formal UN policy machinery, UNFPA should rely more on informal channels and direct outreach to governments, together with the international conference process, to influence national policy. The critical challenge for the UN in policy development is to persuade governments to allocate more funds to population activities, especially to reproductive health and family planning and girls' education programs. Both UNFPA and UNDP should do more to reach out to governments directly and initiate a dialogue with high level leaders. UN conferences have also been successful in engaging high level policymakers in population concerns. It is important to continue these conferences and build on their momentum.

The Commission on Population and Development needs time to grow into its new and expanded role.

Population Action International

IV. The United States and UN Population Activities

American leaders were the driving force behind the establishment of UNFPA.

The U.S. Role in the UN: The U.S. role in UNFPA and the UN's population activities plays out within the larger contexts of both the U.S. relationship with the UN and U.S. domestic politics relating to family planning and abortion.

The United States is the primary financier of the UN system, underwriting 25 percent of the UN's regular budget. Total annual U.S. payments to the UN of some $2 billion, however, represent less than 0.2 percent of the total U.S. government budget of $1.6 trillion. The United States is also the largest single contributor to many UN agencies. UNFPA is unusual within the UN system in that other donors provide the bulk of its program funds. However, the U.S. financial contribution is essential if UNFPA is to expand its assistance to meet the challenges presented by the ICPD plan of action.

Despite Congressional reluctance to meet U.S. financial commitments and responsibilities to the UN, polls show substantial support for the UN among Americans — especially in the roles of improving health and fighting disease, population stabilization, environmental conservation, and disaster relief. Still, critics assert that the United States lacks coherent objectives for the multilateral agencies, resulting in fragmented U.S. policies vis-a-vis the UN.

U.S. Leadership on UN Population Activities: Americans were in the vanguard of the early planned parenthood movement. The United States subsequently led the world in efforts to address rapid population growth and became the largest source of population assistance to developing countries. With USAID funds, private U.S. organizations have built up an unparalleled breadth and depth of expertise in the management of international family planning programs.

From the outset, the United States helped shape the destiny of UNFPA. American leaders were the driving force behind the establishment of the Fund in 1969, anticipating the need for a neutral multilateral organization to work in an area which touches the most intimate aspects of people's

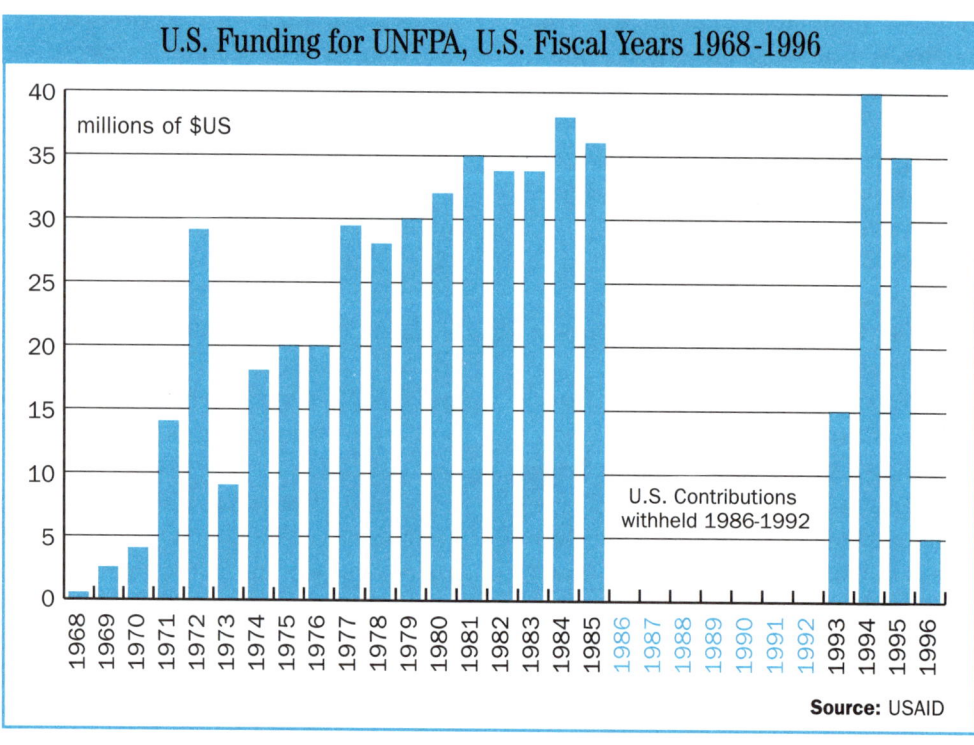

lives. Until 1985, the United States was UNFPA's largest donor, providing nearly 30 percent of UNFPA funding.

The United States was an active player in the ICPD negotiations and played a key supporting role in the achievements of the Cairo conference. Beginning in 1993, the Clinton administration and Congress substantially increased levels of U.S. population assistance. U.S. officials also sought to influence other bilateral donors; during the lead-up to the Cairo conference, for example, they successfully urged the Japanese government to increase financial commitments to population programs.

U.S. leadership and influence with other donors, however, have been undermined by the cuts in 1996 U.S. development and population assistance, including the U.S. contribution to UNFPA. As the United States has the largest economy in the world, cuts in U.S. foreign aid and population assistance and in contributions to the UN could potentially influence other industrialized countries to reduce their assistance.

Political Attacks on UNFPA: The U.S. political consensus on UNFPA began to erode in the mid-1980s, during the Reagan and Bush administrations. UNFPA became the target of U.S. anti-abortion groups because of its program in China, following media reports of coerced abortions in the implementation of China's one child policy. In 1985, the Reagan administration withheld $10 million of the $46 million U.S. contribution to UNFPA approved by Congress. For seven years — from 1986 through 1992 — the Reagan and Bush administrations withheld all U.S. contributions to UNFPA.

U.S. funding for UNFPA was withheld as a result of a legislative provision denying foreign aid funding to any organization that "supports or participates in the management of a program of coerced abortion or involuntary sterilization." Based on their interpretation of this provision, the Reagan and Bush administrations disqualified UNFPA from receiving U.S. support, even though a 1985 USAID review concludes that UNFPA "neither funds abortions nor supports coercive family planning practices."

In 1993, the Clinton administration determined that UNFPA's program in China did not render it ineligible for U.S. funding and restored the U.S. contribution, subject to congressional restrictions prohibiting the use of any U.S. funds to finance UNFPA's program in China. However, through their continuing attacks on UNFPA funding, conservative forces in Congress have undermined the administration and sent discouraging signals about the U.S. commitment.

Although the United States restored its contribution in 1993, the level of funding it provides to UNFPA remains an issue. The annual contribution provided by the United States since 1993 has fluctuated greatly and has not represented any real increase over pre-1985 funding levels. On an inflation adjusted basis, the U.S. contribution had declined significantly, even prior to the drastic 1996 funding cut.

Diminished U.S. Influence: Over the years, the United States has played an important oversight role through its participation on UNFPA's Executive Board. With its great technical capacity in the population field, the United States has provided important input and perspective on proposals that come before the Board. Even when the United States has not been a donor, USAID and UNFPA staff have collaborated on a range of technical initiatives, such as the working group on contraceptive supply.

The funding cuts, however, have undermined U.S. leadership. They send a message of continuing United States ambivalence on the importance

Recent funding cuts have undermined U.S. leadership.

The United States appears to be backsliding on the commitments it made at the Cairo and Beijing conferences.

of population issues and on support for UNFPA. From the perspective of other donor countries and the developing world, the United States appears to be backsliding on the commitments it made at the Cairo and Beijing conferences. As a result, U.S. credibility and influence is likely to diminish in such international fora as the UNFPA Executive Board.

Some other governments also perceive efforts by the U.S. Congress to link its disapproval of family planning abuses in China to funding for UNFPA as disrespectful of fundamental principles of multilateral assistance. The withdrawal of U.S. funds in past years affected UNFPA assistance to all other countries. Moreover, the Fund lacks the authority to terminate an ongoing program of assistance to any UN member state without the approval of its Executive Board—the governments represented on the Board bear the responsibility for all such policy decisions. As a member of the Executive Board, the United States has raised concerns about UNFPA's assistance to China. However, the issue is both sensitive and complex. China is also a member of the Board. In addition, the Board generally makes decisions by consensus, and many other countries have seen UNFPA's presence in China as a positive influence on the Chinese program.

Recommendation #10: **The U.S. administration and the Congress need to adopt on a bipartisan basis a policy of full reengagement in UNFPA, including an increased U.S. financial contribution.** The climate for such an increase is unfavorable, given recent cuts in development and population assistance levels. Still, there are strong arguments for increasing the U.S. contribution: the overwhelming importance of UNFPA's mission to the achievement of overall social and economic development goals; the historical levels of U.S. funding provided prior to 1985, especially on an inflation-adjusted basis; and the relative effectiveness and promise of UNFPA compared to other UN agencies.

As USAID itself has begun to work in fewer countries, an increase in the U.S. contribution to the Fund is important to facilitate the flow of resources to countries where USAID has no significant bilateral population programs, and others where it does not work at all. Finally, it would enable the United States to regain credibility on population issues internationally, and to exert greater influence on the UNFPA Executive Board and on multilateral population assistance programs.

V. Prospects for the Future

The ICPD was a defining and empowering event in UNFPA's evolution. The *Programme of Action* adopted by the conference has given UNFPA not only a fresher and broader mandate, but new energy and direction. Following the ICPD, UNFPA has a more sharply defined vision than ever before. The ICPD has stimulated new initiatives and institutional innovations within both UNFPA and the larger UN system. The current moment is thus a fluid and dynamic time in which the Fund and other UN agencies are attempting to change the ways they have traditionally done business.

A further encouraging development is the emergence of a more self-critical culture within the Fund. UNFPA's top management has already recognized many of the issues highlighted in this report and is striving to improve its effectiveness. Its leadership appears to recognize that, given the Fund's inability to support the more costly components of national population programs such as basic infrastructure, it should focus on advocacy, high quality policy and technical advice, and assistance in mobilizing both internal and external resources. Thus, an opportunity now exists for UNFPA to take a major step forward in strengthening its country-level leadership and programs.

Yet it is difficult to be more than cautiously optimistic. UNFPA's central dilemma remains the dispersion of its limited financial and human resources. To have real impact, it needs more resources but is politically constrained in making the hard choices needed to focus its funds and staff on fewer country programs. UNFPA also needs an enhanced and more diverse base of technical support, together with more complementary working relationships with other UN organizations, especially WHO and UNICEF. Despite the stimulus provided by the ICPD, the Fund still faces many constraints in establishing more effective partnerships with the rest of the UN system. Finally, at this critical juncture in UNFPA's development, the Fund's leadership can no longer count on financial support from the United States — the leader for 30 years in population assistance.

Other nations look to the United States — the world's only superpower — for leadership in solving global problems. The United States cannot walk away from the international accords to expand reproductive health and family planning services and to improve the status of women agreed on in Cairo and Beijing.

Addressing an audience of Americans in early 1996, the Executive Director of UNFPA, Dr. Nafis Sadik, appealed to them "…to confirm your support for the United Nations process, to make good the pledges made in Cairo and Beijing, to maintain your programme of foreign assistance, and in the area of population and development…not to turn your backs on the less fortunate people of the world, among the poorest of whom are women."

The UN — especially UNFPA — has already made an important contribution in the population field. In the aftermath of the ICPD, it is positioning itself to significantly expand its influence on national policies and programs. Meeting global and national population and reproductive health goals will be a long and difficult process, with the needs in many countries far exceeding the resources available. Nevertheless, the UN is an important part of the solution to world population problems — and the United States, together with other donor countries, must support and facilitate its role.

The UN is an important part of the solution to world population problems—and the United States and other donor countries must support its role.

Key References

ap Rees, Garth, et al. *An Assessment of UNFPA's Technical Support Services System.* UNFPA Evaluation Report Number 9, E/400/1995. New York: UNFPA, 1995.

Childers, Erskine with Brian Urquhart. *Renewing the United Nations System.* Uppsala, Sweden: Dag Hammarskjold Foundation, 1994.

Coate, Roger A., ed., *U.S. Policy and the Future of the United Nations.* New York: Twentieth Century Fund Press, 1995.

Conly, Shanti R. and J. Joseph Speidel. *Global Population Assistance: A Report Card on the Major Donor Countries.* Washington, D.C.: Population Action International, 1993.

Crane, Barbara. "International Population Institutions: Adaptation to a Changing World Order." In *Institutions for the Earth*, edited by Peter M. Haas, et al., 351-393. Cambridge, Massachusetts: MIT Press, 1993.

Engberg-Pedersen, Poul et al. *Strategic Choices for UNICEF: Evaluation of UNICEF. Synthesis Report.* New York: UNICEF, 1992.

"Guidelines for the United Nations Resident Coordinator System." New York: Inter-Agency Task Force on the Implementation of the ICPD Programme of Action, September 1995.

Haq, Khadija. "A New Agency for Women." *Planet 7*, no. 4 (1995).

Lee, Kelley, Sue Collinson, Gill Walt, and Lucy Gilson. "Who should be doing what in international health: a confusion of mandates in the United Nations?" *British Medical Journal* 312 (February 1996): 302-307.

Mendelsohn, Steve, et al. *Evaluation of the United Nations Population Fund (UNFPA). Synthesis Report.* New York: UNFPA, 1993.

Pierce, Catherine. *Statement on the Report of the Inter-Agency Task Force for the Implementation of the Programme of Action of the International Conference on Population and Development, 29th Session, February 27, 1996.* New York: Commission on Population and Development, 1996.

Pietila, Hilkka and Jeanne Vickers. *Making Women Matter: The Role of the United Nations.* London and New Jersey: Zed Books, Ltd., 1994.

Power, Jonathan, ed., *A Vision of Hope: The Fiftieth Anniversary of the United Nations.* London: Regency Corporation, 1995.

Sinding, Steven W. "Brief Paper on UNFPA." Paper prepared for Overseas Development Council Congressional Staff Forum Roundtable on Reform of the UN Specialized Agencies, Washington, D.C., April 9, 1996. Unpublished.

Sinding, Steven W and Anna S. Quandt. "Multilateral Population Assistance." Paper prepared for Expert Group Meeting on Population Policies and Programmes, International Conference on Population and Development, April 12-16, 1992. Unpublished.

United Nations (UN). *Report of the International Conference on Population and Development: Cairo, 5-13 September, 1994* A/CONF.171/13. Cairo: UN, 1994.

———. *Review of Population Trends, Policies and Programmes: Monitoring of Multilateral Population Assistance.* "Activities of the United Nations Population Fund." Report to the Twenty-eighth session of the Population Commission. E/CN.9/1995/4, New York: UN, 1995.

United Nations Children's Fund (UNICEF). *The Progress of Nations.* New York: UNICEF, 1995 and 1996.

———. "UNICEF and Family Planning: Background Note on UNICEF Programming." Unpublished and undated.

———. "UNICEF and Women's Reproductive Health." Unpublished and undated.

The United Nations in Development: Reform Issues in the Economic and Social Fields — A Nordic Perspective. Final Report of the Nordic UN Project. Stockholm: Almqvist & Wiksell International, 1991.

United Nations Population Fund (UNFPA). Annual Reports.

———. "UNFPA: Procurement Unit Statistics, 1994." New York: UNFPA, 1994.

———. "Programme Priorities and Future Directions of UNFPA in Light of the International Conference on Population and Development (ICPD)." Report to the Executive Board of UNDP and UNFPA. DP/1995/25, April 18, 1995.

———. "A Revised Approach for the Allocation of UNFPA Resources to Country Programmes." Paper presented to the Executive Board of UNDP and UNFPA. DP/FPA/1996/15, February 5, 1996.

World Health Organization (WHO). "Achieving Reproductive Health for All: The Role of WHO." WHO/FHE/95.6. Geneva: WHO, 1996.

———. "Reproductive health: WHO's role in the global strategy." Report by the Director-General to the Forty-Eighth World Health Assembly, April 24, 1995. Geneva: WHO, 1995.